T0156647

National Union Alliance

A Political Philosophy towards Social Consensus

JACK MEYER

Order this book online at www.trafford.com
or email orders@trafford.com

Most Trafford titles are also available at major online book retailers.

Print information available on the last page.

ISBN: 978-1-4907-9169-2 (sc)
ISBN: 978-1-4907-9170-8 (hc)
ISBN: 978-1-4907-9172-2 (e)

Library of Congress Control Number: 2018912636

Trafford rev.   10/24/2018

 www.trafford.com

North America & international
toll-free: 1 888 232 4444 (USA & Canada)
fax: 812 355 4082

Contents

Chapter One
Assumption and Presumption

Quite obviously, as we go about our daily business it is necessary to make judgments, have opinions, rely on past experience, or simply carry on as best we can as we continually think about our lives. In possessing a set of interrelated beliefs, there exists an underlying assumption that this is enough, that all is well, save in the event of some sort of exception. Happily, for the most part, there is no need to *question assumptions*. Additional thought is not required as that is the very definition of assumption. Unquestionable assumptions are the bedrock of everyday life. Belief in this is the abiding condition of which we are unconsciously perfectly grateful. In one's personal life the prevalent assumption of the priority of "God, country, family, and local football team" serves the needs of the individual and the community. But, when the issue concerns questions of fundamental political philosophy, something more may be necessary, especially when pre-existing political relationships are clearly in trouble. It may become more urgent to take a closer look at prevalent assumptions and more fully consider the underlying circumstances and consequences of commonly held beliefs. In believing, there may be more than meets the eye. In looking deeper, the understanding of one's belief may be radically altered. In a more focused questioning, things may achieve a specifically different meaning.

A certain "halo" effect often exists that encompasses one's beliefs. If an assumption is a specific *content* of a belief, the objective X, as it were, then *presumption* is the emotional affirmation, the "color," the halo, that surrounds and nurtures that X. Easily enough, though, presumption is often felt, or personally experienced, to be more important than the content that is the assumption. The emotional act, the affirmation of *the believing itself,* easily trumps any content X of its choosing. "That is just what I believe. I don't care about any facts!" With this one beholds the essential *rub* that causes social and political sectarian struggle and then violence throughout the world. Unquestioned presumptive belief is waved as the banner of honor that propels one group against any other group's equally unquestioned set of beliefs. In the wake of this struggle, blood often runs deep and wide. "Nobody can know. But everybody presumes. Many are willing to kill without knowing. Without even thinking." [1]

When presumption usurps the function of the assumptive X and therein frees itself from any basis in objective fact and instead affirms itself as self-sufficient then anything goes and there will be hell to pay as evidenced by the historical record itself. The 'truth' is whatever the Number One Chieftain says it is. Any possible benefit from a rational evaluation is trod underfoot as the spectacle of happily marching to war gives way in turn to the grim returning parade of the walking wounded as they shoulder the newly dead. Shrouded in whatever sort of flag and religion only ensures no end to it. The presumption to truth can easily career onto the straightest Road to Hell, pure and simple.

A uniquely difficult circumstance surrounds the effort to determine more precisely the assumptive content X. It is not a singularly discrete objective thing, a sort of endpoint for mathematical measurement that is the signature contribution of the sciences, but rather it turns out that it is something of a *subjectively* constituted reality. The object X may have a footing in the mental processes of human subjectivity, of thinking, as it does not stand alone, all by itself just happy to be recognized as such. In thinking that one thing with another one thing is two things, one begins the mental process towards idealization where the one thing is stripped of its thingness and becomes simply *one,* the primary principle of the science of number, the language of arithmetic, and then idealized yet further into mathematics. *Over time,* this numeric science becomes more and more enhanced and complicated until its original basis in the primary lived reality of one thing and another is *forgotten* and some version of the assumptive content X takes its place. In thinking to have found a final basis in this X there is often the failure to recognize a deeper reality in the unique dimension that is thinking itself. Sorting this out resembles an "infinite task" that may boggle the mind and yet is absolutely essential to any near final understanding. Everything is "on the table" when attempting to think through to the end, until further notice, the reality that is any assumptive X whatsoever. All presumptive belief must be held with the greatest degree of caution. To claim any final knowledge is to ensure no such thing. But, notwithstanding this presumption to a possible knowledge, it is "the way of the world" that precious little of this is allowed to matter. Peoples believe, based upon multifaceted affiliations of tribalism, what they must and then do battle with each other to the final death, calling it honor or whatever misnomer that deflects the truth as their relative gods have already forsaken each other. The battle in the name of tribal deities can never end well. But some effort must be made to do just a little better, to think through beyond the limits of specific tribe, even if against all odds.

A further difficulty emerges that compromises any effort at final understanding and that is that there may be no such thing as final understanding. In contrast, while mathematical questions may find a final answer, political questions resist such precision and some sort of *compromise* becomes necessary. Based upon various relative presumptions, a search for consensus is possible only *if* desired. A *political* solution occurs when parties to the fray choose resolution, yet seldom is this the case as the "fight to the finish," winner take all, is the best that can be done. After long years of struggle, any tribe may see its best interest served in the flames of a final destruction, compromise be damned. The "last best hope" of mankind is for the alliances of moderation and tolerance to prevail over the partisons of extremism and intolerance, a heavy burden in the very best of possible circumstances when reality is surely far worse.

Any attempt to get to the evidential basis of a reality based political philosophy must work through these layers of presumption and assumption as only then would it be possible to attain a clearer political insight. How to begin? Is such a theoretical project possible? Why go there? Who cares? Some would claim the need to let the default political situation play itself out and let the winner take all. The game of presumption vs. presumption has been engaged, let it run its course. Survival of the fittest. The potential damage done though could involve a return to the Stone Age, certainly a humbly experience for most of the few survivors.

Preliminarily, a more precise definition of the term political is necessary. Common usage narrowly defines it as anything to do with the process of getting elected to public office, the many ways in which the voters are brought to their senses so to speak, and then casting a vote on one person's behalf. "Forget the facts, just vote for me, I'm a winner, be a winner too!" A million variations on this theme are imaginable to fit any occasion. In the manipulation of the electorate to one's own elected advantage one has engaged in the political, as pseudo-celebrity journalism would have it. If civil society is essentially the *balance* between the community and the individual then the proper definition of the political is the science of attempting to establish that balance with respect to the specifics of human life. The individual must be encouraged to thrive within the context of the greater responsibilities of the community. Law is established to insure a mutually beneficial result, where both individual and community do better. The current search for balance is disrupted as the entrenched interests of the Left (community) and the Right (individual) pushes for an exclusive advantage that diminishes the other. Only when each recognizes the reciprocal benefit of each to the other is the domain of the political more properly understood. The other is not the enemy but rather the completion of the half that each must necessarily be. What is a tree without its leaves or a leaf without its tree? Not much. When the principle of personal initiative and the principle of the social safety net mutually sustain each other then there is something recognizable as the balance between the Left and the Right where the Center emerges in full view. In an affiliated way, the entrepreneur may start a business but its workers are needed in order to carry on and finish the work. Each working at odds produces nothing, while together the stated goal becomes possible. Mutual respect is the clearest "race to the Top," when the race to the bottom is so often the case. The fashionable political "winner take all" mentality does not understand its own benefit through the agency of the other. A final "victorious" Left or Right signals the absolute demise of each. *Short-term* personal advantage consumes itself.

Stated otherwise, while the pursuit of the assumptive X is fraught with difficulty, there is a foundation of fact that is clearly evident if one chooses to look. Social reality is comprised of the interrelationship between the individual and the community and only within this dynamic is individual life possible. Finding the balance between the One and the Many, the person and the community, is the primary task of political thinking. There is no undefined assumption or emotional presumption with this, the facts are clearly evident.

As a simple thought experiment perhaps there is a way to begin, a way to do more than just continue the status quo, a way to think clearly with less presumption and assumption, a way to care about more than what has narrowly served one's long established and deeply held partisan emotional beliefs.

What would be some presumptive assumptions that could possibly cause political confusion and trouble? Two such essential assumptions push to the front. Each causes America to indulge in failed policy that goes without question. The first is that "all men are created equal" and the second is that "democracy is a universal value." In reality both of these assumptions fall far short of the evidence, as each then leads political judgment astray into continued failure in many ways. One at a time. The varying circumstances at birth dictate something much less than equality. Who and what are the mother and father? On the one hand the alcoholic mother will give birth to an alcoholic child who will grow up with every sort of physical, mental, and social disadvantage. On the other hand, are the physically fit and emotionally prosperous mother and father who choose to give their child every possible advantage. Being born into these vastly different worlds cannot equate to equality. Simply, "all men and women are created unequal." The belief in equality is a self-edifying presumptive assumption but a belief only as it accordingly has nothing to do with the circumstances of reality. The United States Constitution is based upon this erroneous assumption. Political policy easily runs aground with this discontinuity of belief and reality. In the general pursuit of happiness the idea of equality has no chance at all as factors of social status, inheritance, and privilege drive the outcome to the advantage of the few who once established in power relinquish nothing. Much has been decided in advance. Social policy that hopes to impose equality "from above," as well as after the fact, can only fail. A shorthand formulation may be useful. For example, in educational social policy, assuming equality, the standard of results is that children ought to be ready, willing, and able to function as productive citizens. But the facts of reality intrude. Some surely are ready, willing, and able but some are unready, willing and able and some more are unready, unwilling, and able and the rest are simply unready, unwilling, and unable. The template of equality cannot work with this. In the game of life, the winners and losers, for the most part, as exceptions are possible, are determined in advance. But few are the exception. A safety net that does not enable the rest entrenches profound social inequality that will end in the holding tank that is prison.

The cruel irony is that the preordained "winners" affirm their "earned" superiority as the equally preordained "losers" are self-righteously accused by the "winners" of moral turpitude or just laziness and therefore worthy only of rightful condemnation and neglect. No Brother's Keeper here. Assuming universal equality facilitates this difference of judgment as the "privileged" strut their phoney superiority and proclaim the legitimacy of their heavy burden when there in fact has been none.

A further example of the failure of the assumption of universal equality concerns the circumstances surrounding the issue of the minimum wage. When assuming equality, the specifically unequal "winners" assert that their success is *exclusively* the result of their initiative and effort. The winners then take all the credit and assume that the losers are equally responsible for their failure, giving them the exclusivity of blame. The fact of fundamental inequality cannot enter into this self-serving interpretation that then insures further "cheap labor" for the winners' businesses and frees those winners of any responsibility for all those who have "lost." When wages are minimal and inadequate of a possible living, then so be it, as that is the consequence of the failure of personal responsibility. The natural bias, inequality, of the system is the inconvenient truth that can never be acknowledged. Ideology trumps reality and further damage is visited upon the land. An emerging "new" America may be patterned after the "sharecropper" or plantation systems of prior years as the vested interests simply impose their economic advantage and demand of the vast majority a life of scarcity and squalor, the finish line in the race to the bottom. In the richest country in the world, is this the best that we can hope for? This fundamental disparity drives in the direction of social discontinuity and the increasing prospect of a civil war. Any "winning" with this would be an equal losing.

The second assumption that coaxes American foreign policy into a bedeviling series of mis-understandings is the presumptive belief in "democracy as a universal value." In rightful pride over its relatively successful democratic experiment Americans presume to unilaterally export this to the world over. What has been sucessful for America will surely be welcomed throughout the world. What could be more obvious? But democracy (even if it does exist in America, being so biased by plutocratic money) is an extremely difficult cultural accomplishment that is very unwelcome and essentially inconceivable in many areas of the world. The global predominance of multi-faceted *tribalism*, whether theocratic or ethnic, mitigates perfectly against any implementation of democratic principles. Primarily, tribalism could be defined as the social unit that embodies the principles of exclusion rather than any possibilities of inclusion. One is *against* far more than what one is for, and this is emphatically consolidated by history and tribal tradition. The singular characteristic of tribalism of whatever local flavor is its affirmation of the *advantage* of the strongman, the chief, who dictates from on high and must necessarily impose his will backed by the threat and fact of violence. There will always be the "Gestapo." To paraphrase the great French tribal chieftain Louis XIV, "I own everything and everyone." All power emanates and is imposed from above. There is to be no middle class, those secure in their relative independent prosperity, as there can be only the welfare of the King. Without the institutional structures of civil society where rule of law and the protection of individual rights are well established, there will be no prospects for democratic formation. There will be room for only one opinion. The Rule of One crushes the rule of Law. American foreign policy that hopes to impose democratic institutions from the outside is as dunderheaded as it will insure casualties. Holding an election in a newly "democratized" client state that *votes along tribal lines* obviously has little to do with the civil society necessary for democracy. But American policy makers are easily convinced of their self-serving rhetoric. The United States often gets involved, in democratic "nation building," on the wrong side because there is no right side. Again and again in the name of democracy many very bad things are done with few apologies after the fact. Long existing tribal hierarchies will never relinquish their power because some American "do-gooders" hope to impose democracy.

Another presumptive belief that continues to sully the political debate is that "government is the enemy." One can quickly rejoinder with the obvious fact that "the only thing worse than bad government is no government," go ask all the failed states everywhere. Governments in name only are well in place throughout the world. Rightful criticism would be more useful if directed at making bad government better. The chanting rant that is in search of the "end of government" is as goofy as it enhances the profits of a "shout-journalism" that can only put a quick spin on something that contributes less than nothing to the rightful goal of legitimate political reform. The profound value of liberal democratic government is that it maintains the civil society, the institutional structures, that allow for the possibility of rational social and economic behavior. When those of a contrary view are not taken out and shot everyone is better off. People will necessarily disagree on specific things but equally fully agree on a general underlying consensus that insures equal protection for all. Civil society, so easily taken for granted, is the greatest accomplishment of the Western spirit and is to be cherished and not denigrated for purposes of short-term self-aggrandizing hysteria.

☆ ☆ ☆ ☆ ☆

This introductory foray into the realm of definition is intended to establish a starting point that begins with the calling into question the many presumptive assumptions that are taken over all around without further consideration. But we must proceed with an open-mindedness that is often unavailable to those intent upon political rancor and division. More specifically, what is intended is a specific *attitude* that allows for the full range of political possibility, as it forecloses upon the narrow sectarian ideology that simply hopes to "win" at any cost to the common good. A balanced and rational discussion would be the hope while maintaining a dispassionate view that could possibly end in insight and grace.

Summarily, with the entry into political judgment it is necessary to adhere to the principles of careful definition that in turn requires an ever clearer understanding of presumption and assumption. Any relatively mature political appeal must stand upon legitimate reality and not some fiction cut from the cloth of self-serving wishful imagination. Political judgment sullied by vested single issue special interests that are intent only upon the narrowest view is the perfect formula for a grinding political failure and eventual collapse. An alternative view, based upon evident political principles, is here offered towards the possibility of a Middle Way.

Various calls for the creation of a "Third Party" have generally fallen short as they are envisioned as a sub-party attached to either extreme of the Big Two. In contrast to this there stands at the Center a place where true legitimacy becomes possible based upon a demographic abundance.

Chapter Two
Principles and Demographics

Perfectly evident is the fact that the American social and political system is in crisis. Irresponsible, short-term, and special interest "thinking" coalesce into a toxic formula that sickens all around. Political party leadership drives the fray and yet again spins the tired, worn, and self-serving ideologies that deliver advantage to only the well positioned few. Deep seated problems escalate further and continue a slide toward predictable catastrophe. Nothing is allowed to be done to the contrary. Existing political alignments serve the interests of the narrow-minded as the broader interests of the nation are left wanting. Presidential and Congressional power struggles have been reduced to the level of "petty tyrants" defending a personal political turf at all cost. The drive for elected office trumps any possible *rationality* of political philosophy.

Republican and Democratic squabbling is virtually devoid of underlying civil respect. The individual interests that drive these parties are self-serving to the highest degree. The Right and Left continue to reiterate ideologies that lack any sense of the common interest. There can be only the specifically special interest. Furthermore, media requirements demand immediate reaction, as there is no longer accorded the time for reasonable analysis. Necessary and detailed discussion cannot occur in this climate of political chaos where the personal hunt for national power consumes all energies. Voters are promised that others will be called upon to pay for the benefits to which they have been convinced that they are entitled. In a world of such mean spirited contention it is perfectly logical that nothing of merit be allowed the light of day. Fundamental problems are left to fester and then worsen. The average person is without cause for optimism. While it is easy to point to others as the root cause of the problem, we too, *all of us*, are party to this contention and accordingly must consider our own responsibility. We have gotten what we deserve, as each has been "paid off," as it were, by any number of special interest "gains." It is necessary to re-think our political situation in the spirit of reasoned discourse.

How is it possible to think about these things? How are we to think in a way that transcends partisan ill-will and that would approach a level of both national consensus and natural cooperation? The problem is that it is difficult to think in any terms that are not already engulfed by the "politics of the next election." The personal desire for the power of elected office is simply too great and addicts like a drug. What passes as "thinking" quickly reduces to little more than the ideologies of small-mindedness. Political party operatives are thinking about getting their man elected so as to maintain their own position of power in the bureaucratic hierarchy. Political think tank thinkers, those charged with thinking through the rationality of irrationality, are thinking about the general virtue of their own specific way of thinking, never choosing to question their own assumptions.

> The scholars at most public-policy institutes today . . . are chosen for their views, not their expertise, and in any event, know the conclusions at which they must arrive. They are not explicitly

pushed toward any views but they understand that
they were not hired by these think tanks to be free-
thinking intellectuals.[2]

Furthermore, the structured discipline of academic thinking
leaves that thinking fragmented and divided, as each "field"
affirms its own knowledge to the discredit of any other. The
specially positioned field of philosophy ought to call upon
itself for a general and philosophical thinking yet it is the most
fragmented of all and speaks in a jargon and minutiae that could
interest only the few. Journalism is naturally driven by the single
day's events and is therefore without the perspective and time
needed in order to think more deeply. And, finally, the rest of us
must think about making a living. By *default*, then, it remains
to the politicians and their operatives, think tankers, academics,
and journalists, the opinion makers of the world, to do our
thinking for us. And therefore, of course, we get exactly what
we deserve, and *a crisis is now upon us.* Certainly, many of these
opinion makers offer much that is constructive and informed,
but failure arises when there can be no conscientious attempt at
historical and philosophical perspective, where partial answers
are muddied by the force of circumstances, and where little effort
is made to do better. The worst of it reduces to a *shout-journalism*
that is sold as reasoned analysis, but all that remains is fractured
and fragmented views and personal animosity that lend clarity
and insight to nothing. Generally, all of these partial views
could be summarized as irresponsible, self-serving, and short
term "presumptive assumptive affirmation," or a calculation that
knows little of reason, nothing of reciprocal consideration, and
perfectly without balance.

Ironically, it may be the statistician, the pollster that does
most of our thinking.

Politicians, corporations, and journalists spend
vast amounts of time, money, and energy trying

> to divine the public's views on everything from
> Social Security to the afterlife to carbonated drinks.
> It is a race, actually, to be the first to genuflect
> before them. Pollsters have become our modern
> soothsayers, interpreting public opinion surveys
> with which their predecessors read chicken entrails.[3]

Polling then is a "counting" that calculates the desires and wants of the mass electorate and then hoping to tabulate the straight road to elected office and forward to the consumption of the public spoils that is its just reward, its entitlement. Simply there is no thinking at all but only a pretense that veils a thinner and thinner "truth" or, the Big Lie. Thinking needs to find a way in which to reach beyond the hidden agenda of political operatives, the limits of academic discipline, and the narrowness of hurried journalism. Something different is required. Thoughtful re-consideration must be possible that is in the *best interests* of all. Common sense must be the guide and our first responsibility, but the task is not easy as "everything is always easier than to exercise common sense."[4]

Compounding and further entrenching our system of political gridlock is the transformation of Congress into multiple "fiefdoms" of personal power that leave individual Congressmen on the perpetual wheel of "re-election." "From an institution dominated by 20 or so powerful leaders, Congress has evolved into a collection of 535 independent political entrepreneurs who run the system with their individual interests uppermost—i.e., to get re-elected."[5]

Under the heading of National Union Alliance (NUA)[6] a tentative alternative will be presented. With only a *shift in attitude*, it is possible to envision a radical change in political perspective. A simple formulation can establish a beginning. On the basis of principle, agenda, and policy, *center Democrat and center Republican have more in common with each other than each have with their respective extremes.* Accordingly, it would be possible to build on this intentionally ignored consensus as the basis of a *Center Party*. At this middle ground, this in-between, a political agenda could be considered that is free of the polarizations of the Left and the Right. Immediately an observation would become evident that there are no longer any "Center Republicans" at all as radical political "simplism" has driven everyone to the far Right extreme or out of the political sphere entirely. Centrist Republican Congressmen have suffered systematic defeat at the ballot box. Be this as it may, while the ideological politicians have run to the far Right, the electorate itself has not. Some few have followed Republican leadership but the greater majority have remained Center Right in spirit as that is where their final best interest resides. This group simply now lacks political representation.

A diagram of general distribution may be useful. The political spectrum from the far left to the far right can be represented with the deviation of the Bell Curve. The area between the curved line and the horizontal axis represents the general distribution of any given statistical group, applied here to political society as a whole. The curved line extends both to the far left and right. Area C extends from -1/4 to +2 and would represent the Republican Party. Its varied agenda begins to the left of the center line and then extends far to the right. Area D would represent the Democratic Party and reverses the area of the Republicans and extends from +1/4 to -2. The range from -1/4 to +1/4, Area B, represents the area of shared agenda, *the area where bi-partisan consensus is taken for granted.* This is the place where Republicans and Democrats quietly agree. Not surprisingly then, both the Left and Right *overlap* respectively a bit to the opposite side of the center line, as each embraces *some* of its apparent opponent's ideological turf. Generally, uncontested matters of the "nation" and issues of mutual self-interest would occupy this middle ground. But in the ongoing and never-ending battle of Left vs. Right, none of this is to be acknowledged, since to be seen as cooperating in any way with the "opposition" is not to be tolerated. Partisan division must be made to reign supreme. Power is won by fostering differences rather than by acknowledging natural consensus. Of course, both the Left and the Right have moved far away from any Center overlay and each continues to "rule" its domain from their respective bastions of extremism. Each has forsaken a natural demographic abundance at the middle for a diminishing scarcity at the fringe.

NATIONAL UNION ALLIANCE

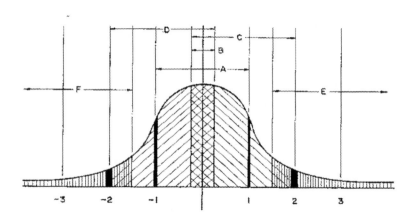

A *National Union Alliance*
B *Bi-Partisan Center*
C *Republican Party*
D *Democratic Party*
E *Right Wing Fundamentalisms*
F *Left Wing Socialisms*

The extent of right wing fundamentalisms is represented by Area E, from +1 ½ to 3 and beyond. Being aligned to the fringe of the Republican Party, this *far* right is able to influence and aggravate agenda and policy to a much greater extent than its demographic numbers could ever justify. On the other side, the extent of left wing socialisms, Area F, from -1 ½ to -3 and beyond, aligned to the *far* left of the Democratic Party, is able to influence and aggravate more than its numbers could ever justify. The heated emotions of extremes disrupt any possibility of consensus, as the self-satisfied *experience* itself of such emotions is the highest "political" priority. This *heat* galvanizes the political experience and keeps cash flowing briskly into the party coffers. To orchestrate high moral outrage is to loosen the purse strings of those who can be expected to give. The proposed political party of the National Union Alliance would break with this traditional alignment of polarization and look instead to the middle. It would build upon the natural consensus of the *bi-partisan Center* and encompass the area designated as A. Center Democrat and Center Republican could be re-oriented towards each other leaving their respective fringes to begin life anew on their own, where emotions are quickly spent and resources easily exhausted. The majority of concerned human beings would see that their best interests as both individuals and as members of the larger society are better served with this agenda at the Center, *in-between* the Left and the Right. With the isolation of the political extremes, this newly constituted majority could lead with coherent authority. Fundamental decision-making would become possible. Historically it has been true that elections are won through the emotional agitation of extremes but true governance is possible only at the Center. It may be time to consider the possibility of winning a national election based upon the political principles that stand at that Center.

The middle ground carries great potential. Not ideologically enfeebled, most people would naturally choose a reasonable middle course. When proper evidence is presented it is possible to sift through and then select an agenda that reaches toward balance and mutual respect. It no longer need be the all or nothing of ideological impasse but rather a reasonable accord of differing interests. It is the difference between those who have decided everything in advance and those who would rather have recourse to evidential truth. And herein lies a distinction of greatest significance. Evidential truth very seldom reaches to the standard of "absolute" truth, as it necessarily remains "good until further notice." The emotionally enforced close-mindedness of political ideology will not tolerate such open-mindedness, as truth is best dictated as "final." But the real world *sprawls* elsewhere and it is our responsibility to think as best that we can when at the same time recognizing the possibility of continuing evidence to the contrary. Truth finding is a process, not an assertion of absolute fact and accordingly policy and agenda must be open-ended and positively enhanced by further development. Life is a matter of a series of choices that have particular consequences within a network of multiple relationships the results and truth of which no one can foresee. We must do our best and then do it again. The attraction to fixed ideology is of course the fact that all of this messiness and uncertainty is immediately foregone in the absolutes of belief. But responsible thinking is ever so much more complicated and any reduction to a set belief simply an intellectual violence that can easily convert to a bloodier version elsewhere.

So the *NUAlliance* is not intended to convince those who must necessarily always refuse, but rather it hopes to orient, organize, orchestrate, and then finally marshal the forces of "The Middle Way" towards the possibility of concerted action on behalf of all. Traditional philosophical attempts to understand the reality of social life have been based upon the absolute and relative importance of the individual with respect to the community, that is, the philosophical question of the proper relationship between the One and the Many. Rehearsing this central topic, some theories propose the priority of the individual but most assert the priority of the "state." The question is one of individual rights versus state rights. As all of this has come down to us, and then taken root in American liberal democracy, the issues have become confused and contradictory as philosophical theory has given way to ideological battle. But the essential element remains the same. What is to be the *region of balance and legitimacy* between the prerogatives, the rights, of the individual and the requisites of the social whole? The political strife of recent years has been caused by the proponents of either one or the other imposing its interpretation of this question, wherein a "hidden" agenda of a particular special interest is usually the real motivation. Both ideologies will promise great reward for some few individuals. Well-heeled minorities are usually set to benefit. But the results are never clear-cut, as neither side, the Left nor the Right, is able to unilaterally dominate and the *net effect* is that a "standstill" occurs. Intelligent discussion cannot be heard above the din of ideological double talk as the possibility of consensus government is reduced to the gridlock of mean-spirited contention. Partisan initiatives are intended to fail in the hopes of achieving the "victory" of self-righteous moral outrage. The Presidential veto and Congressional filibuster becomes the expression of "leadership" as all that remains is to assert a final rejection and to say "No" to everything whatsoever. Many experience a somewhat ironic joy as they feel vindicated and "martyred" by political defeat. Outside of the political process, the rest of us are left free of any ability to positively act on our own behalf. Nothing is to be done.

It is time to consider a possible break with this tradition of irrational exaggeration. Standing at the center of the political philosophy of the NUA is the understanding of the *equal and balanced* validity of both the individual and the social. Each must be understood primarily with respect to the other. Individual rights are possible only within the limits of social responsibility. The individual is the primary basis of human life yet there are absolute social requirements to which the individual must defer. The individual must be free unto himself, but the social must have the right to limit any behavior that is in conflict with the natural rights of others. The essential principle of the possible balance between the person and the encompassing world of others then is the person's own *self-responsibility*.

What, more precisely, are the positions of the ideological Right and Left? Who are the ideological Conservative and the ideological Socialist? Standing at the very center of each position is a particular belief regarding "agency." The Conservative believes in the absolute priority of individual agency whereas the Socialist believes in the absolute priority of social agency. The one defends the rights of the individual whereas the other affirms the requisites of the social. What renders each an "ideological" position is that neither will recognize the middle ground where each would achieve a *balance* with respect to the other. Each exaggerates its own virtue at the expense of the validity of the other. Each sees only itself and is blind to the appropriate fact of the other.

An essential example may illustrate this point. The issue is taxation. The Conservative's belief in the absolute priority of the individual entails the additional belief that *taxation is a subset of theft*. The government, in this view, therefore has no right to collect taxes and does so only as a violation of individual rights. What is not understood though is that it is governmental institutions that *create the possibility* for any person to earn anything at all. Courts, police, integrity of markets, law, etc., simply, the entire structure of civil society, are governmental institutions that must exist before anyone earns anything. The consequence of this is that taxes are not theft but rather must be rightfully collected in order to make economic activity possible. On the Socialist side, the belief in *entitlements* entails the additional belief that someone else's taxes must be collected in order to pay for the entitlements to which so many have been led to believe are their natural right. Predictably, the Conservative is ever in pursuit of a tax cut as the Socialist seeks to maintain ever expanding entitlements. Neither position, of course, has much to do with reality. "Taxation as theft" is simply wrong-headed and "entitlements" quickly exhaust anyone else's ability to pay. An ideological position is asserted that renders mutual accord inconceivable. Each is wedded to its ideological position as mutual "demonization" renders all possible discussion towards political consensus meaningless.

As a consequence of their essential ideologies, the Conservative believes in *inequality* and the Socialist believes in *equality*. Human abilities are different, as some few persons have extraordinary ability and merit, as many more have less. The Conservative therefore believes in a natural hierarchy of ability, merit, and position, and it is this difference that allows some to choose to do more and some to choose to do less. Leveling this difference is useful to no one. But the Socialist disagrees and believes emphatically in equality. *All men are created equal,* after all. As a person, no one should be valued more than any other and only equality ensures that no one is taken advantage of by any other. Each has equal rights that are to be protected under the Law. Naturally, each of these positions, the inequality of the Conservative and the equality of the Socialist, are exaggerations of fact. As self-conscious agents of productive activity we are obviously unequal and yet as persons we must be equal. It is again the recognition of the *balance* and tension between the two that allows one to see the reality of the world as such. Each position is an exaggeration that denies the appropriate reality of the other. They are not mutually exclusive but rather two differing ways in which to understand the single reality of human life.

Both are right for the wrong reasons. Each believes in the *absolute* validity of the one or the other, when in reality each is what it is only *relative* to the other. Inequality is unequal only relative to equality, as the criterion of merit establishes a hierarchy of more and less. Simply, some people do more while most do less. Equally, equality is what it is only relative to the criterion of the sameness of a human being with respect to another. Some can and do, some can and don't, and some can't. The principles of inequality and equality then serve as the relative *exception* to the rule. If the rule is one then the exception is the other and vice versa. The *political* question then is one of attitude, or the presuppositions from which one begins. Everything is equal and unequal relative to equality and inequality. One is left with the middle ground, the *in-between*.

Partisans of the Right and the Left, the Conservative and the Socialist, have each inappropriately elevated their respective preferences of inequality and equality to the dimension of absolute "principle," and therein becoming blind to the natural priority of the truer principle that necessarily underpins each. Ideology is born of this misapplication of definition and any further "thinking" succumbs to the many ways in which an ideology may be imposed. It frees one of the effort of thinking as it equally frees one to the emotions of partisan politics and its divisive personal aftermath. Nothing more need be questioned as the rancor of division clearly finds its way to the front as civil hatred pushes closer to civil war.

From these two ideological positions, human agency and inequality for the Conservative and social agency and equality for the Socialist, are spun out a multitude of beliefs and unbeliefs, affirmations and disclaimers, and reduces to the demonization of all else but oneself. Both are blind to the full density of the middle ground as each more tightly grasps the rather meager residue of pure ideological belief. This serves the emotions but misses the mark entirely of the reality of our shared world and the possibility of legitimate governance.

It may be possible to learn from the wisdom of the ages. "Once upon a time I heard a statement made which has just this moment flashed across my mind. It was that nothing is so hostile to like as like, none so hostile to the good as the good . . . by a universal and infallible law the nearer any two things resemble each other, the fuller do they become of envy, strife, and hatred . . ." [7] Have we not reached the level of collective maturity where it is possible to overcome this dislike of those who ought to be our closest friends? With the very most in common (language, country, history) we have chosen to aggravate our relatively minor differences to the point of pervasive disdain. This has been our choice as it all along could have been otherwise.

Returning to the principle of self-responsibility, fashionable sociological-psychological theory will disclaim the validity of the person's self-responsibility, claiming instead that no one is free at all. The material forces of nature establish a causal necessity, so it is asserted, that leaves no place for the possibility of personal choice and that, therefore, there is no such thing as the "person" at all but rather only an aggregation of material "tendencies." Accordingly, there is no holding the person accountable for his deeds and no consequences ought to be imposed for any damage that must necessarily follow. The naturalistic bias of modern psychological science must be turned on its head and give way to the higher criterion of *common sense*. "It's fashionable to explain away crime as the result of environment and upbringing, always putting the blame on someone else, never the actual culprit. No one's born bad, all that sort of thing. If it weren't for poor housing, violent father, unemployment, capitalism, et cetera et cetera." [8] "Actions had to be accounted for and responsibility accepted. Consequences had to be faced. *Constant forgiveness destroyed the soul . . .*" [9] The reality of self-consciousness and self-responsibility stands at the very core of our being and is the essence of *who* we are, as we find ourselves already within the community of others. This is not a "material tendency" but rather the consummation of a universal spirit. It is this alone that defines the essential aspect of being human. Without this, without the spirit of self-conscious awareness, there can be only a material determination. Without personal choice there is only animal existence, that peaceful unconcern about anything at all, that mindless "chewing of one's cud" that relives itself the very same, moment to moment, day after mindless day.

Stated more directly. Twin boys grow up to be utterly different. The one is an alcoholic and claims that he was so "because his father was a drunk." The other was a man of integrity and accomplishment, a clear personal success, and he claims that it was "because his father was a drunk." In other words, upbringing may be a factor but not the *deciding* factor. Each achieved the Age of Reason, when each could choose who each is to be, and one chooses drunkenness and the other something quite different. As with us all, we choose ourselves *regardless* of all else, even if that "choice" falls to a default condition of thinking oneself *not* to have chosen. We each are what we have finally chosen to be.

In freely choosing, we decide to build, to create, and to think about the opportunities before us. In the act of choosing, we are able to build a future that is different and better than the one of the past. Sociological and psychological theory cannot account for this astounding and marvelous difference. The inertia of material force can produce only *less* of itself, but nothing different. The denial of self-responsibility is just the hope to offer an "excuse," to become a victim, so as to avoid the consequences of freely chosen failed responsibility. The social, economic, and political system pays a dear price for these excuses. Positioned at the middle, the NUA would constitute true accountability, balancing the individual and the social, the One and the Many, so that neither is able to deny its full share of responsibility.

If self-consciousness and self-responsibility serve as the central philosophical principle of the NUA then a second principle concerns the necessity of understanding that the common interest takes natural priority over the special interest. This is not to suggest that a special interest is without political rights but only that it must remain *secondary* to the primary *common interest*. The immediate difficulty of course is the determination of this common interest, as generally the many special interests often try to pass themselves off as if they are indeed not special at all but rather embody the very ideals of the common interest. Single issue political factions easily delude themselves into this intentional confusion. This is taken as being normal as no one is able to speak from outside the contention of never-ending ideological struggle. With the possible political re-orientation to the Center, as envisioned by the NUA, it is hoped that a rational voice will be heard from outside that struggle and that that voice will be heard with persuasion and authority. Only then will it become possible to forge a consensus as to a more precise articulation of the common interest. Freed from the emotional ideologies of division, it is possible to reach forward to a common understanding. The "noise" of current political contention has never given this a chance but the time is now appropriate to enter into this dialogue.

> ". . . we must learn to distinguish between individual decision making as expressed in market behavior and collective decision making as expressed in social behavior in general and politics in particular. In both cases, we are guided by self-interest; but in collective decision-making we must put the common interest ahead of our individual self-interest. I admit that the distinction is not widely observed. Many people, probably the majority, follow their narrow self-interest even in collective decision-making. It is tempting to throw up our hands and join the crowd, but it would be wrong, because it would hurt the common interest. If we really believe in a common interest, we must recognize it on our part even if others do not recognize it on their part. What distinguishes intrinsic values is that they are worthwhile irrespective of whether they prevail or not." [10]

A companion principle of the priority of the common interest is the priority of the long-term interest over the short-term. A perfectly clear criterion is at work. Given any issue, simply project 20 years and decide if the "numbers" would be tolerable or even conceivable. Policies that serve the moment at the expense of the long term could be described as self-inflicted disaster, a slow and willful suicide. Pushing problems out yet one more year, or one more election cycle, constitutes a final calamity, as vengeance surely will be delivered. But political thinking must be short-term and votes gotten *now,* and that is the end of it. With the fact of a forthcoming election, people are prodded to vote their own short-term special interest, as their payoff must be immediate. Looking to the long-term, the stellar example is the continued accumulation of the Federal Debt. This looming monster reaches out to a "tipping point" where payments are no longer sustainable or even possible. The social crumbling of potential default will reach a point of no return and the world as we would hope it to be will no longer be possible. We will have chosen the irreversible return to the Stone Age. A balanced and reducing Federal Budget needs to be put into place, enacted for the common good. Effective action needs to be taken now, but stonewalling and refusal is the norm and the short term happily reigns supreme. Another example, at its current rate of increase, will health care be affordable in 20 years to anyone at all? Something different must be done now with the comprehension of this certain fact. Grid-locked into the politics of irresponsibility and special interests, the long term good is sacrificed to the need that must be paid now. Is this the very best that we can do? Can we only stand by and do nothing on our own behalf? Are our divisions so great that it is judged better to sacrifice the future world simply to maintain a satisfaction of always needing to say "No" today? The newly touted Affordable Care Act (ACA) has entered the fray with an inherently damaged product that hopes to change everything while changing very little as the vested special interests continue to hold sway.

Three principles then stand at the center of the NUA: self-responsibility, the priority of the common over the special interest, and the priority of the long-over the short-term interest. What justifies these three principles? They are simply self-evident, obvious in a way that common sense would easily recognize. But more can be said. Everything that makes personal life worth living is the result of one's self-awareness and then the ability to act in a responsible way. If this is denied, then human life remains at the level of non-conscious, simple and immediate existence. But through thinking, self-consciousness, and self-responsibility, one is able to place oneself in one's world as a free individual, free to think and act as one sees fit. The great cultural edifice of society itself is rooted in the collective deeds of thinking and responsible human beings. Fundamentally, then, free political life is meaningful and coherent only when the responsible person stands at the center and when social relations are maintained that support that person. Necessarily, each person must participate in a responsible way but general welfare is possible only in the context of social reality as a whole. One must act as an individual but can live only in the greater reality of social relations. Accordingly, the common interest naturally takes precedence over the special interest of the individual. Now, certainly, the individual must be protected from the possible overreach of the common interest, but when matters of policy are considered the common interest must have priority. No individual or special group is greater than the social totality; no part stands larger than the whole.

> Coercion is natural; freedom is artificial. Freedoms are socially engineered spaces where parties engaged in specified pursuits enjoy protection from parties who would otherwise naturally seek to interfere in those pursuits. One person's freedom is therefore always another person's restriction: we would not have even the concept of freedom if the reality of

coercion were not already present. We think of a
freedom as a right, and therefore the opposite of a
rule, but a right *is* a rule. It is a prohibition against
sanctions on certain types of behavior. We also
think of rights as privileges retained by individuals
against the rest of society, but rights are created
not for the good of individuals, but for the good of
society. Individual freedoms are manufactured to
achieve group ends. [11]

Often lost in the political hubbub of self-interest is the
recognition that one's final interest must be mutual respect.
When any narrow view is pushed to its final and logical
conclusion, there is the attitude of civil war. In the emotional
heat of partisan politics, there is still understood that a general
conflagration can be in no one's best interest. One's political
opponent may be one's adversary, but he is not one's mortal
enemy. In the end, it may all be just a game of personal gain but,
when squared with total loss, the limits of the game have been
reached and recourse back to the middle ground welcomed. "Let
both take the middle course." [12]

While these three principles stand at the Center of the
political philosophy of the NUA, a fourth principle, or reality,
is required. This is the simple *will* to think through this re-
consideration and then to choose to act accordingly. The
personal will of the individual needs to be invoked to the
highest degree in order for the *courage* of political transformation
to become possible. One needs the courage to *see* that this is
possible and then step forth into the void of the untried in
order to achieve something new and better. The person needs
to bring himself to "look to the Good" and re-make himself
on the threshold of the positive. Idle theory must be resolutely
transformed into political action, as thought must be made
to inform human reality. It is the question of choosing more
rather than settling for less. But the questioning is difficult and

any answers tentative at best, "good until further notice," as it were, but nonetheless the attempt is necessary and worthy of our greatest effort. It is now possible to turn to specific details.

The specific policies of the NUA agenda would naturally divide into the three areas of international relations, domestic relations, and budget and taxation.

Chapter Three
International Relations

The status of the American military going forward is central. It would be *retracted* from its advanced positions throughout the world. The United States needs to get out of the business of running the world; it should leave regional problems to the local players and quit intervening where its objectives are both confused and self-serving. A significant role remains as a cooperating partner but it can no longer bear either the cost or the responsibility for the difficulties and failed choices of others. Generally, then, the policy of the NUA towards international relations would be one of fairness and economic cooperation in a context *freed of the military option*. The attitude of the unilateral would be replaced by the affirmation of the multilateral, and the maintenance of a single center of power would be replaced by its de-centralization. The United States would seek to find its appropriate place in the world rather than being determined to fix into place all others. America could display world leadership by relinquishing its attitude of global domination. The critics (foreign policy elites) will charge that this is but a new "isolationism" and, consequently a proven failure, but the issue concerns more the possibility of "minding one's own business." The notion of running the world through Washington is no longer a possible objective. The United States cannot "do it all" when in so doing it simply creates its own enemies that could only be expected to push back. Wars are ongoing simply because the American military is *there*. This is not an isolationism but rather a new clarity of understanding that recognizes the limits of power. The body bags returning home are as unnecessary as they are the end result of choices freely made.

A specific example of this military retraction would be the full return of Okinawa to its rightful owners the Japanese and therein quit with the constant prodding of the Chinese. Treat someone like an enemy and that is surely what they will become. *Go ask the Athenians.* [13] American military presence in the Middle East is the single greatest cause for continued hostilities. Get out of an area where one is both unwelcome and despised. The presumed hegemonic global authority of the United States can no longer be sustained and is being contested sharply in many areas. Standing down would encourage others to stand up to legitimate responsibility. Continued American arrogance in this regard may cause its own demise.

The United States then should retract its over-extended military position throughout the world. It should bring its troops and equipment home. It should recognize that the military option is no longer acceptable or appropriate. When so much is spent on the military option, it becomes so easily *the first option*. The billions of dollars that would be saved would accelerate positive transformation elsewhere.

At the same time, Cold War bureaucracies need to be re-constituted. The Central Intelligence Agency (CIA) was created as a Cold War institution and has produced "documentation" that supported every step that escalated tension. The CIA has a history of "inventing the numbers" for any President who felt moved to "contain" Soviet power. With the collapse of the Soviet Union, it has come to light that CIA estimates were consistently inflated and intent upon continuing the stalemate. The CIA's central "product" is often simply exaggeration. It has done the most in giving to the world the face of the "ugly American." Its role would be re-thought as "smaller." Its recent failure with respect to Iraqi estimates confirms its inability to "tell the truth." Its activities in Iran in 1953 (Operation Ajax) created a disaster which drives events yet today. The narrow interpretation of "self-interest" as the projection of American power is a policy that has formed the bedrock of assumption for so long that no one can see that it is the single cause of continued failure. (Few would even know what Operation Ajax involved, namely, the dismantling of a functioning democracy and it replacement with a despotic tyranny, but a tyranny warm to American dictates.) The time tested assumption of policy no longer works and is the very cause of continued and increasing global instability.

With this military retraction, the role of the Pentagon bureaucracy would be reduced. Having been in charge of the military implementation of the policy of "containment, counterforce, and counterinsurgency," all of which no longer has any place in global relations, the Pentagon ought to be scaled back proportionately. The Cold Warriors need to be retired as a group as their biased views infect ongoing policy. The dead vision of cataclysmic division needs to be buried. The Cold War mentality that still grips the Pentagon is one of history's great anomalies. The implosion of the Soviet Union that completely changed geo-political reality did nothing to alter the ideologies of those in charge. Vast carrier groups and schools of nuclear submarines still patrol the world stalking a prey that has vanished. Policy still perpetuates a bureaucracy that refuses to give up its place in a world that is no longer served by its presence. The Neo-Cold Warrior simply wants to make the world an American province for the sake of power and domination. Resistance will be forthcoming. The military-industrial-foreign policy complex is a self-sustaining and self-absorbed bureaucracy with diminishing objective justification.

Many live off of an ideology of the threat of perpetual warfare and strife that must necessarily require their services. Clinical psychology has a name for this, simply insanity, or just nuts.

How does this policy of military retraction square with the three principles of the NUA? In being more faithfully responsible to itself, the United States ought not take on the failed responsibility of others. Tribal conflict throughout the world is the responsibility of those involved; it cannot be mediated through Washington. It is not the United States' responsibility to correct the problems of the world, as it is hard-pressed to address its own. Secondly, the common interest is best served by the retraction of the United States military. The wasted billions could be allocated elsewhere. Some budgetary relief is the first positive. The military bureaucracy itself has become a special interest, which hopes to perpetuate itself at the expense of others when its "mission" has diminished in a changed political world. Thirdly, retraction easily serves the long-term interest. To continue to waste resources on massive military structure into the future would be perfectly insane and would accelerate economic failure everywhere. No longer needing to play the part of a military superpower, it would be possible to re-direct resources to the task of building a better world for all. It is difficult to imagine a more appropriate or attractive alternative.

The events of September 11, 2001 changed the world forever and any suggestion of a retraction and reduction of the American military would be seen by many as foolhardy and simply woefully naive. The longstanding projection of this military presence throughout the world has caused specific opposing reactions that trigger actual military action that then sets into place a recurring cycle of action/ reaction that spirals towards greater and greater destruction. It is with this that the full extent of American *complicity* can be recognized. In hoping to subdue so much of the world to its own interests, the American busybodies have created and maintained a legacy that is resented and finally despised.

When reaction finally comes from those rendered seemingly powerless, the damage can be profound. With nothing more to lose except their lives, the suicide bombers line up for their last best hope at redemption. Notwithstanding, though, it is not single events but rather long term policy that has created the conditions for terror and violence. The imposition of American will to power will be resisted. Without accepting and acknowledging the fact of this complicity, the American policy elites feel entitled to impose a level of violence that is without limit. They simply do not see any other point of view and do exactly as they please. But, in exterminating one generation of terrorists, one simply spawns the *naturally more numerous next* generations.

Re-stated in others terms. The forward positioning of the American military is often the initiating cause of difficulties, which it is then called upon to be the solution. It is not a neutral presence whose force is imposed impartially, rather this presence mobilizes opposition and it can only be perceived as being a "bully." Many tolerate this presence and accept American hegemony (usually having been "bought off") but for others there can be neither toleration nor acceptance. This presence invites attack, and then the cycle of retaliation begins, moving from forward presence, to local attack, to massive retaliation, to heavy civilian casualties, to more accusation, to recrimination, and on and on, reiterating the same as the emotions of self-righteous justification square off against the emotions of victimization and hopelessness. The *cause* of all of this may be an American policy that places its military as an *invitation* to trouble. In a world of profound confusion, misunderstanding, and blind hatred it invites *big trouble*. Patrolling with "the big stick," the Americans may feel secure and self-assured, but history is replete with examples of comeuppance due and then delivered. When this all comes to grief, the Americans may easily blame and accuse others but a less self-serving look would reveal inherent complicity and a profound lack of self-understanding.

"An awareness of the way one is perceived by others is an indispensable self-correcting mechanism."[14]

A glimpse into the future gives reason to pause. If American military power chooses to fully square off with the Islamic world then the prospects are poor. It is the difference between a very large target and none at all. The great Western economic system is as powerful as it is vulnerable to easy attack. As the American military looks for smaller and smaller targets with bigger and bigger payloads, the Middle Eastern terrorists will find bigger and bigger targets that can be easily hit at the leisure of their choosing. The "daisy cutter" may be dropped over and over to no avail as the smallest "pinpricks," suitcase bombs, trigger mass panic and destruction everywhere. It will be the panic that will do the most damage. America may think it can win such a war with all of its might but it is precisely this might that most readily exposes it to piece-by-piece destruction. A lesson may be taken from oncology and the "life" of cancer. The malignancy consumes its all-powerful host a little at a time and at the leisure of its own choosing. Its only purpose is the consummation of perfect destruction and final death. To be is not to be.

America may already have chosen the path to this self-willed destruction, this engaging an implacable foe that desires only continuous devastation at the time and place of its own choosing. The greater the military domination, the more surely will that military come to grief. Its mission to destroy will return home as the millions that have now become its new enemy will infiltrate, interfere, sabotage, and finally blow it all to Kingdom Come.

Is the West being *baited*? Has it been drawn into a drama that portends its own demise? Convinced of its righteous invincibility, Western power, as projected by the American military, may be being enticed to inadvertently choose its own annihilation. The alternative is to retract and give less cause to the next ready generation of suicide avengers. The alternative is to re-consider the entire range of policy that has brought us to this impasse. The alternative is to consider the middle ground, the in-between. ". . . once on the tiger's back, we cannot be sure of picking the place to dismount . . ." [15]

In any battle between dramatic unequals, the more powerful must always lose. The degree of vulnerability and the size of the target make the random shots of the less powerful deadly accurate. The struggle between American might and Islamic terror will finally be decided in the attrition of pinpointed attacks. The greatest power on earth simply will have nowhere to retaliate. David and Goliath easily come to mind in the battle of big versus small as the big is indefensible against the small. All advantage goes to the opposition. No colonial power remains any longer standing over their overseas "possessions" as each were dispatched in turn by the inability of its power to be worth much at all. The United States did not win in Vietnam.

Things may be even worse than this. In needing to specifically respond to a single horrendous event, American policy precluded itself from recognizing the larger context of the circumstances in play. This context of course involves general American policy in a part of the world where it simply does not belong. In other words, the need for a single response narrowed the discussion to military force *as if* that were any discussion at all. America may have unwittingly created its own ongoing domestic threat of terror as it hoped to return terror elsewhere. Furthermore, this single response would need to be "telephotogenic." In marshaling domestic support, the conflict would need to "play well" in the category of television journalism. The war needed to be won back home, as emotionally sustaining support would be essential for carrying the war forward. The needs of journalism then dictated the terms of the discussion, which of course is underpinned by the need for ratings and advertising dollars. This leaves one in the unsettling position of thinking that the American policy of war is dictated by the need to sustain consumer consumption. Ironically, this may bring us very close to the essential motivation, excess American consumption in the form of Middle Eastern oil.

In sanctioning the emotional need for retaliation, American policy descends to a raw senseless emotion. "The man who seeks revenge digs two graves." [16]

Chapter Four
Domestic Relations

In tandem with the retraction of the American military, domestic social policy would be equally re-constituted. But, before turning to the details of policy, it is necessary to make a clear statement *in the defense of governmental institutions*. Recent fashionable political ideology has made a great fuss about the incompetence and inefficiency of bureaucratic governmental institutions. All the problems of the nation and the world, so it is proclaimed, are to be attributed to these institutions, with the clear remedy being their systematic demolition. Yet, a closer look reveals something quite different. Governmental institutions are not the essential problem; rather it is the failure of political administrative leadership that leaves these institutions less than what they should be. A few examples will suffice. Based upon this accusing ideology, the United States Department of Agriculture (USDA) is perhaps as big, inefficient, and misdirected as any yet the American food supply is the most plentiful, varied, and affordable in the world. The Federal Aviation Administration (FAA) manages the skies that are crowded with thousands of aircraft and millions of passengers and throughout all of its possible incompetence there is a safety record that is simply impressive. The Social Security Administration (SSA) manages a universal benefit program with impressive efficiency. Critics may point to areas of concern, but no one could reasonably question its general accountability and success. Those who condemn most viciously are also the first to condemn the *lack* of institutional structure when disaster strikes and the institutional "safety net" is missing. "How did the government allow this to happen? And they better pay for my losses!" The hypocrisy is as wide as it is deep. Bad government is infinitely better than no government.

Regulatory agencies of all sorts provide a judicial structure that establishes the conditions for the possibility of a fair and open marketplace that protects the many participants from the cartel-like grasp of criminal overlords. Without legitimate and enforceable rules there can only be the deadly free for all of the advantage of the stronger. The reduction and lack of effective government terminates in the endgame violence of tribal carnage.

Furthermore, when the critics of "big government" achieve the Presidency and take power, becoming the rightful caretakers, they generally underfund, understaff, and undermine. A self-fulfilling prophecy is set into place where institutional structures *are specifically made to be* inefficient and sabotaged of their proper capacity. The possible long-term damage to effective liberal democracy is incalculable in advance but, if these institutions should fall, the ensuing "tidal wave" of social destruction will startle even the most self-righteous of earlier hypocrites. Of course they may be lucky enough to have been swept away with the initial deluge that will leave only a few pathetic survivors.

Such governmental bureaucracies need no longer be ideologically condemned but instead be understood as providing the *essential* institutional structure that allows for the possibility of civil society and, more particularly, liberal democratic society. An easy comparison illustrates the obvious. Many countries throughout the world *lack effective* institutional structure and then are necessarily immersed in civil chaos. The Soviet Union's demise into the various states that have Russia at the geographical center are successful or not precisely with respect to the presence or absence of these institutions. Russia can barely manage itself, being unable to collect the taxes that are its legal and rightful due. Furthermore, it cannot sufficiently police itself to gain advantage. Without institutional control, what remains is a social "survival of the fittest" that quickly reduces to the savagery of post-modern tribal warfare. When institutional structure is lacking, there can be no civil society, as the well armed and naturally divisive "tribes" take their bloody conflict into the streets. Only effective governmental bureaucratic institutions can begin to insure the individual rights of citizens. The acquired right to condemn government is the result of the legitimacy and success of that same government.

Political ideology that chooses not to understand and appreciate this fact, that fails to see the development of Western governmental institutions as the very condition for the possibility of civil society, is simply misguided. Such ideology does not understand that its constitutionally protected right to criticize has been guaranteed by the formation of the very institutions that it so freely condemns. The partisans of the Right, who affirm the rights of the individual with such rancor and acclaim, need to understand that only in a civil *institutional* society are such rights possible. Without it there can be only the hierarchy of tyranny that will tolerate no rights whatsoever, ready examples of which are to be found throughout history and the world today.

What is necessary is *balance*, equilibrium, between the individual and society. The many partisans of unfettered individual freedom take for granted the value of institutional structure and finally promote the demise of civil society itself. With that of course is destroyed any individual freedoms at all as a plunge into tribalism can only end up in the "advantage of the stronger," or despotic tyranny.

Finally, then, when considering social relations from the perspective of the political philosophy of the NUA, the principles of self-responsibility and the priorities of the long and common interest over the short and special interest, it is necessary to appreciate the central role that governmental institutions must play. Within the domain of Social Relations the essential piece of all policy would involve health care and its possible reform. It is where tremendous resources are being consumed and where changes to individual behavior would result in the greatest benefit. It is also where fundamental difficulties plague a failing system, a system that simply has no capacity to either grasp or address the larger issues. A health *insurance* system that cannot insure 50 million people is in need of structural reform. Only a governmental institution would have either the scope or ability to begin to handle such a *universal* problem. In simplest terms, ". . . everyone of working age shall pay a weekly allowance premium, then gets benefits when they are sick, unemployed, retired, or widowed." [17]

Health care reform would logically begin with a single payer system. Private health insurance companies simply are not able to deliver efficient health care management on a universal basis. The profit motive of these companies establishes two principles that run counter to quality-inclusive care. Profitability is based upon the exclusion of as many people as possible and the denial of as many claims as possible. Locked into the mentality of exclusion and denial, private insurers cannot achieve the level of care and efficiency that is necessary. Since private health insurance companies *contribute nothing* to the actual health process, concerning themselves only with the collection of premiums and the payment of claims, a single payer system would be vastly more efficient, a task easily handled by a "bureaucratic" institution such as an expanded Medicare.

Money would be paid as payroll deductions and as a broad based National Sales Tax. Claims would be paid directly based upon established criteria. Equally, the "profit" of private insurers is better allocated to health care itself. The ever-increasing power of computer software programming renders great efficiencies of scale. The natural duplication of competing companies doing the same thing compounds final costs. Ever increasing insurance executive bonuses can easily be seen as having little medicinal value.

A common mantra of the Right is that all problems would be made better through the imposition of *competition*. But how is competition even possible with the collection of premiums when that is all that one is doing? If health care *costs* are determined and controlled by others (hospitals, doctors, big pharma, etc.) where is the competitive possibility? There is none. A single payer system of health care delivered and money collected and then paid, based upon consensus criterion, is significantly more efficient than any presumptive competition. Cooperative efforts rather than competitive profits are better suited to the issue of universal health care.

A critically important fact also is that the true cost of medical care over *the full length* of a person's life is never determined. In other words, private insurers "take all the good risks," the young and the healthy, and leave to the government the cost for all the "bad risks," the old and the sick. It is this that is the fundamental indictment of private health insurers. Their profit making effectively dumps onto the Federal Government the bulk of medical care costs. Common sense then counsels in favor of the virtues of a universal plan. Only the self-interest of ideological blindness will not see the necessity of a plan of general care that is based upon true benefits and real costs. A new bureaucratic institution of this magnitude and importance can be successful if only given a chance, if only allowed to exist without interference and sabotage by those who would feel presumably better if it were to fail. Those who value profit above all else will not be happy with this but that must be their own quite personal affair as the general welfare is the concern of those who would choose to do better.

Any insurance executive would admit if honestly forthright that his insurance "paradise" would be the largest possible pool of participants with the most inclusive demographic distribution, spanning the youngest to the oldest, thereby providing the greatest precision in the calculation of risk that would then allow for the most equitable determination of individual premiums. The many payers would pay the naturally fewer receivers such that over the course of a person's life the cost-benefit ratio would be equalized. Payments in would be balanced by payments out, without the distortion of "profit."

The fact that 50 million people are without health insurance coverage does not mean that they are simply excluded, rather they will incur medical costs that will generally go unpaid and then must be *absorbed* by the system as a whole. The escalating cost of the medically uninsured ripples through the economic system in many ways. For example, a primary cause for personal bankruptcy is unpayable medical bills. A *universal* system of payment then insures that some of this cost will be recovered. The possible change to such a universal system would meet with immediate disapproval, as examples of the "failure" of other "nationalized" systems, would be offered. But the simple fact is that a universal plan will not be any worse and has the potential of being better. The existing patchwork system is providing for *some* but for *many* it is quickly disintegrating into unaffordability, denied claims, and finally, no care at all. The disturbing hard irony is that to purchase health insurance is no cure, as after the fact, after the occurrence of a medical claim, the insurer may simply reject the claim, denying coverage. Now try to collect. One doesn't know what one has purchased with a health insurance policy until it turns out that there was no coverage at all. In the realization of this doom there is simultaneously a zoom in company profits. It's a shell game that one can only lose. A single payer system is the only rational alternative. It would require leadership and a political *will* in order to make this work, but *it could be done*. The essential virtue of a universal plan is in the details and not in any ideological first impression, and to those details we must turn.

The concern over health care touches upon many aspects of social life but everything starts with the individual. It is crucial that each individual contribute to the cost of care as only in this way does protection become affordable universally. The individual would pay a percentage, say 5%, of gross income as a payroll deduction in the manner of the Social Security payroll deduction. The employer would pay a smaller percentage, say 3%. An annual deductible would apply of perhaps $500. In this way *business would be freed from the fury of uncontrollable health care insurance costs* and yet at the same time would contribute a reasonable amount. Equally, the individual would come to know the real cost of care. With existing programs the individual is "sheltered" from such information and merely expects that any medical costs are to be paid by someone else. When the care recipient knows nothing of cost and is without any responsibility of payment, that cost will naturally escalate higher and this without any escalating benefit. Costs simply rise when no one cares otherwise. Business bears a far too heavy a cost for the health insurance of its employees. This plan would remove that burden and then at the same time spurring greater employment. The greatest obstacle to the hiring of more people is the legitimate fear of the punishing cost of health insurance premiums. Corporate America ought to be the first constituency to line up for this switch to universal coverage.

Adverse individual behavior would incur *an additional premium* payable by the individual alone. For example, tobacco users would pay an additional premium. Convicted alcohol related motor vehicle violators would pay an additional premium depending upon the severity of the offense. Those already paying higher premiums for adverse behavior would pay a higher deductible. Simply, a health care *partnership* would be enacted where the cost to the individual would be determined by that individual's personal choices. Adverse behavior would pay more because it costs more and responsible behavior would pay less because it costs less. People would be encouraged, *not forced*, to choose the better and less costly life style. When the financial incentives are sufficient perhaps there would be reason to pause and re-consider. For example, the smoker may decide that the misery of his addiction is no longer worth the added cost.

An essential clarification is necessary. Not all of possible medical costs would be covered by this plan of universal coverage. The Federal Plan, extended Medicare, would not cover those things of relatively limited value, such as organ transplants, chemotherapy of proven limited results, and all those things that are monstrously expensive, on the "cutting edge" of medical science, that dramatically distort health care expenditures. Way too much can no longer be spent on just a few.

The fundamental principle though is that of self-responsibility, as *the person is left with choice.* Through these kinds of financial incentives the individual would be encouraged to make healthy life choices. This would influence behavior for the better but would primarily be a way of collecting money from those who will end up costing more to the health care system. A whole range of disincentives could be considered. The principle is that adverse behavior, for which the individual is responsible, would be charged an additional premium. When "bad" behavior costs significantly more some may find within themselves the motivation to change. In comparison, for example, the strategy of suing tobacco companies for damage done to willing smokers, while emotionally gratifying, is misplaced. There may be some corporate responsibility, but it is obvious that it is the person who possesses the final responsibility. The choice to smoke is the person's alone. After the fact, after years of self-inflicted damage, one need not hold anyone else responsible. Only a befuddled legal system would entertain even the possibility of this sort of suit. To be sure, tobacco companies have made handsome profits in the marketing of ugly death but it is the person who must be held accountable for their own suicidal behavior. Much higher tobacco taxes would address this question and put smoking further out of the reach of children.

General health care strategy then would change. The allocation of the health care dollar would be shifted *from cure to prevention*. Society implicitly encourages a person's choosing the "low road to slow suicide" and when death is imminent a half million dollars of high tech medical machinery is thrown at the patient with the best hope of extending that life but an hour or two. Exaggeration, yes, but essentially true. This strategy is a failure and none the less so for being the accepted and highly profitable norm. Modern medical science holds up the prospect of an eventual cure for conceivably all of human disease but the cost is astronomically high, while the true and virtually *free* "cure" to most disease is prevention. Large sums of money naturally go to the interventions of cure. People do little to help themselves, yet finally feel entitled to the resources of cure when surely it is already far too late. The quickly escalating high cost of health care is directly related to the choice of the strategy of cure. Life long health and well-being though is one's own full responsibility at virtually no cost at all. It is with the attitude and personal resolve of prevention that well-being is immediately there.

> It's a matter of record that health care costs in the U.S. are up to around one trillion dollars a year. Of that horrendous figure less than 2.5% goes for prevention and an even smaller amount—a mere 0.5%—goes for health promotion; leaving approximately 97 cents out of every health care dollar for treatment; which is about everything from basic first aid to extremely costly intensive

care. Nothing is spared to treat the injured and
diseased.[18]

Prevention then is the key for lowering health care costs
and raising health wellness. Another name for prevention is
self-responsibility and it is only this that will make any real
difference. A high authority says it well.

> People smoke and wonder why they get cancer.
> People ingest animals and fat and wonder why
> they get blocked arteries. People stay angry all their
> lives and wonder why they get heart attacks. People
> compete with other people . . . and wonder why
> they have strokes. The not-so-obvious truth is that
> most people *worry themselves to death.* Worry is just
> about the worst form of mental activity there is—
> next to hate, which is deeply self-destructive. Worry
> is pointless. It is wasted mental energy. It also
> creates bio-chemical reactions that harm the body,
> producing everything from indigestion to coronary
> arrest, and a multitude of things in between. Health
> will improve almost at once when *worrying* ends. [19]

> All illness is created first in the mind. [20]

What obstructs though is the Western health (sickness)
system itself. It is not the sick as patient but rather as *consumer*
that is essential. The high cost of Western medical intervention
requires that equally big money be paid. The system is naturally
biased towards the more costly procedure.

> . . . doctors in the West deny the healing efficacies
> of doctors in the East because to accept them, to
> admit that certain alternative modalities might
> just provide some healing, would be to tear at the

very fabric of the institution as it has structured
itself. [21] . . . doctoring and politicking have become
institutionalized, and it's the institutions that fight
these things, sometimes very subtly, sometimes
even unwittingly, but inevitably . . . because to
those institutions it's a matter of survival. [22]

While the institutional problem is deep-seated, nonetheless it
remains the choice of the individual, both patient and doctor, to
choose otherwise for themselves. Prevention is the health giving
choice that is all one's own. The virtue of fasting also would be
promoted as having proven to produce significant benefit across a
variety of ailments. With no cost at all better results are possible.

Coupled with the failure to mobilize the power of prevention
is the inverse mobilization of huge amounts of money in order to
artificially and mechanically extend the natural end of life. There
is no "cure" but only a merciless mechanical extension of life. "A
quarter of all health expenditure in the United States . . . is now
spent on patients during the last six months of their lives." [23]
No good can come when the natural limits of life are artificially
extended and the personal dignity of the individual violated.
People must be accorded the dignity to die when that can be
their only hope. Some would charge that this is nothing less
than "playing God," this refusing to mechanically extend life,
but it may be more aptly understood as "playing the Devil," as
it imposes an evil and suffering rather than any possible benefit.
"The entire medical profession is trained to keep people alive,
rather than keeping people comfortable so that they can die with
dignity." [24]

. . . in America, every effort is apt to be made
by a materialistically inclined medical science to
postpone, and thereby to interfere with, the death-
process. Very often the dying is not permitted
to die in his or her own home, or in a normal,

unperturbed mental condition when the hospital has been reached. To die in a hospital, probably while under the mind-numbing influence of some opiate, or else under the stimulation of some drug injected into the body to enable the dying to cling to life as long as possible, cannot but be productive of a very undesirable death, as undesirable as that of a shell-shocked soldier on a battle-field.[25]

The health care industry then would be transformed by the philosophy of prevention and the mercy of allowing people to die when that is their only wish. Both of these would save vast sums. The power of self-responsibility is at its very greatest when individuals choose to do better of their own accord. "I did see, in a way, though I had never before thought of death as a welcome quest to be patiently awaited, hoping that he would come quietly, when one was asleep." [26]

Health care in America is twisted in a profound way by the contrary objectives of the institutional "players" themselves, something that only can be addressed by the implementation of a Universal Plan. The food industry wants to preserve the right *to kill you slowly* as does the pharmaceutical industry. Government, in the form of a politicized USDA and FDA, often stands aside and applauds the profits made, which makes some few very happy. One example among many will do. Aspartame, the sweetener of choice, is a toxic poison that should never have been brought to market and yet it pervades the food and beverage industries. Its toxicity destroys neurological functions, memory and thought processing, and finally reduces people to chronically debilitating and degenerative diseases. Rather than spending billions to find the "cure" for Alzheimer all one need do is ban the use of aspartame. Any legitimate cost/benefit analysis would ban such an insidious killer yet now nothing is done as profits are to be made. A Universal Plan would do this cost/benefit analysis as it is the payer of last resort and it would immediately rule against such an intentional profiteering at the expense of general health and well-being. Those proclaiming the evil "socialism" of a Universal Plan are those involved in the existing industry that affirms the right to kill you slowly. With the philosophy of prevention comes the call to do everything better, to facilitate health and well-being regardless of the profiteering interests to the contrary.

Perhaps nowhere else is the possible social and political *balance* between the individual and the community better showcased than in a refined notion of the Single Payer system. When individual responsibility is set as the cornerstone of social benefit then the advantage is mutual. The individual maintains his or her responsibility, *or not*, and the social benefit is calculated accordingly. There is no "free lunch" as a personal responsibility is the first principle.

Civil society's attempt to enact a law in order to "solve" a problem often instead imposes an even greater problem or, simply "the cure is worse than the disease." The premier example is the American prosecution of the so-called "War on Drugs." The machinery of the War delivers a lethal level of destruction that far outpaces the damage of any possible personal drug use. With the mandate of law and the assurance of the moral superiority of the mission, Federal policy prosecutes a war that is out of control and out of any proportion to the problem. The billions spent are wasted. It is a "gateway" policy that ends in perpetual casualties both at home and abroad. It is the *illegality* of drugs themselves that is the far greater problem than drug use itself. This War is the "big muddy" that will engulf ever more victims forever and ever. There can and will be only failure, and then the continued escalation of cost and casualties. "It is corrupting everything it touches."[27] As *a different strategy for control and prevention*, the use of "controlled substances"

would be de-criminalized. This is not to promote, encourage, or condone usage, but rather is an attempt to *replace* an obviously failing policy of enforcement.

> Had drugs been decriminalized crack would never have been invented and there would today be fewer addicts . . . The ghettoes would not be drug-and-crime-infested no-man's lands . . . Columbia, Bolivia, and Peru would not be suffering from narco-terror, and we would not be distorting our foreign policy because of [it]. [28]

Any consideration of such a dramatic shift of policy would be initially met with a huge outcry of objection but if discussed outside the confines of narrow interest and ideological rancor, it is possible to understand the clear benefits of this change of policy. But one need no longer be oblivious to the obvious. We have been so conditioned by the rhetoric and incantations of the "War on Drugs" and assured of its absolute necessity, or suffer the horrible social consequences, that rational discussion is not allowed. But the other side of this War is intriguing and worthy of serious consideration.

The use of drugs is essentially *two* problems. It is a matter of the activity related to its production and distribution, on the one hand, and the negative health effects occasioned by its use, on the other. The high profits of distribution drive the criminal element and reduce cities into turfs of "tribal" warfare. Without profit, criminal distribution would disappear.

> Legalization of drugs would reduce crime in the ghetto, and much that is positive would follow. The vast majority of the crime network ought to crumble. The importance of that cannot be underestimated.[29]

Violence on American streets and throughout the world, such as in Columbia, Mexico, and Afghanistan, would virtually vanish, as that violence is causing more death and destruction than the drug use itself. The virtue of this "revelation" needs to be fully comprehended and pondered. De-criminalized drug sales would be heavily taxed, creating revenues for programs of prevention and rehabilitation for the individual. Simply, by removing the profit from the sale and "pushing" of drugs, the problem of social violence would be diminished. Reduce the unit cost from say $100 to $1, add $4 in taxes, and a very large problem is solved. By breaking the drug problem into two parts, it would become easier to manage and control each. Criminal violence would be greatly reduced and forthright programs of prevention increased. The emerging social benefit of this is nearly unimaginable but it is there for thoughtful consideration.

> The only thing that keeps drug prices high is that drugs are illegal. When legal, the marketplace will soon dictate the proper price. That people have been willing to pay outrageously inflated prices for drugs indicates they would also be willing to pay outrageously inflated taxes on drugs. Yes, some people will abuse drugs (as they already do), and drug abuse will have its costs to society (as it already does). Drugs, however, unlike cigarettes, will be able to pay their way—and create a significant amount of government revenue. [30]

The bravado of militaristic type talk in the end simply justifies governmental sanctioned violence. The heavy rhetoric of "drug war" and "czars" is without meaning and is merely deadly idle talk.

> The goal of legalizing drugs is to bring them under effective legal control. If it were legal to produce

and distribute drugs, legitimate businessmen would enter the business. There would be less need for violence and corruption since the industry would have access to the courts. And, instead of absorbing tax dollars as targets of expensive enforcement efforts, the drug sellers might begin to pay taxes. So, legalization might well solve the organized crime aspects of the drug trafficking problem. [31]

With legalization would come the enactment and enforcement of mandatory drug testing laws in the workplace. It would be a person's right to purchase and use drugs but an employer's right to have a drug-free work environment. Drugs would be legal to buy but their use would jeopardize a person's livelihood. Many more people would make the choice to "just say No." Simply, legalization, the elimination of the criminal element, treatment, and incentives for non-use, would all greatly limit the debilitating effect of drug use on society as a whole. Furthermore, the current "War on Drugs" is not worth the life of a single more law enforcement officer. Legalization would go a long way towards protecting those whose job it is to protect others. It is asking far too much for these people to risk their lives in the pursuit of murderous drug dealers. Individual drug use would be reduced through proper treatment and rehabilitation. Those who choose to get their "fix" could do so at a lesser cost to society rather than at the astronomical cost that illegality incurs. Give the addict his daily dose for $5 rather than $500 and the level of burglary and assault would naturally plummet. The problem could be contained in a way that its current profitability does not allow. At its worst legalization could not be any more damaging than the present "war" and it would cost much less. This War is simply "a dog that won't hunt."

The legalization of just marijuana would create a productive renewable industry. There are two types of marijuana, one containing sufficient THC, the active agent, that is smoked, and the other, hemp, that has little THC, but its fiber is immensely useful. Under existing law, hemp is lumped with marijuana and therefore a perfectly benign plant is banned as contraband.

> Whereas trees—currently our primary source of paper—take twenty years to grow, hemp can grow to be twenty feet tall in a single season. Warm climates can produce three hemp harvests per year. This, obviously, makes hemp a far more efficient plant for producing paper than trees. In addition, making paper from hemp—unlike wood pulp— doesn't require acid, so all hemp paper is 'acid free' and thus lasts for hundreds of years. Hemp could supply virtually all of our paper, cardboard, and other packaging needs. [32]

As farmers look for new products, it is possible that they grow hemp for the vast papermaking industry. Precious forests would no longer need to be leveled.

The medicinal value of marijuana is well known.

> Marijuana is the best medicine for reducing nausea in people being treated with chemotherapy. Marijuana is also an excellent treatment for glaucoma, which is responsible for 14% of all blindness in America and affects 2.5 million people. Marijuana has also been proven effective in treating asthma, epilepsy, MS, back pain and muscle spasms, arthritis, cystic fibrosis, rheumatism, emphysema, migraines, reducing tumors, and in promoting appetite. [33]

This may be somewhat over-stated, but nonetheless positive medical benefits are a fact. While hysteria and special interests have claimed the addictive nature of marijuana, the evidence points elsewhere. There is simply no proof that it is addictive even though some of its users will go on to other drugs. The critical fact is not its presumed addictiveness but rather the choice of the individual, for which that person is *absolutely* and solely responsible. Simply, with the legalization of just marijuana a productive, beneficial, and tax paying industry would have been created which would replace the War on Drugs. Use would not be any greater and the cost to society would be dramatically less.

The move towards legalization may be quite simple. It is a question of money. "A group of powerful, white, middle-aged men will meet in a room to discuss what to do about marijuana . . . and they will reach the only logical conclusion: tax it." [34] In any battle between moralizing hypocrisy and profit, it is profit that will win. In a budgetary climate of ever diminishing resources, it will become perfectly obvious that the ready cash of legalization is infinitely preferable to the ever-escalating cost of a "War" without any conceivable merit.

The legalization of drugs has far reaching social consequences. It raises the question of the criminalization of all acts between and among consenting adults. There is no authorization for the jailing of these "criminals" from either the United States Constitution or the Bill of Rights. A crime is an act that violates the rights of either another person or his property or, simply, *an act that has a victim.* "Crimes" of consenting adults have no such victim and, consequently, the highest law of the land prohibits governmental intrusion into these activities. If Constitutional principles are to stand, then all "crimes" of consenting adults must be repealed. Laws against gambling incur the added factor of hypocrisy. It is simply a person's right to do what he wants with his own money, if there is no violation against anyone else. The media carries the betting line and many games of chance legally prosper yet a certain few bring police, lawyers, courts, and prison. Again, the gains to society with rational legalization as compared to an irrational, hypocritical, and spotty criminalization are immense. The process that finally ends in prison is infinitely more costly than a process that immediately pays taxes. Let the gambler have his Constitutional right and he will gladly chip in to the public coffers. The hypocrisy would be less.

Some estimates claim that 350,000 people are currently in prison for committing acts between consenting adults. An additional 4,000,000 arrests are made yearly. [35] The numbers are astounding in terms of what could be saved if the "government got off the back of the people." A recent Senate "Crime Bill" carried on the hypocrisy. It can "think" only to put more police officers on the street and build more prisons. It should, instead, empty the prisons of 350,000, and eliminate 4,000,000 arrests. But leadership is lacking.

> Politicians today tend to follow popular beliefs
> (even if those beliefs are based on prejudice,
> inaccuracies, and myths), repeat the popular beliefs
> back to the populace (thus enforcing the prejudices,
> inaccuracies, and myths), and make laws to support
> the popular beliefs (thus institutionalizing the
> prejudices, inaccuracies, and myths). Some say it's
> democracy. Actually, it's cowardice. [36]

A national consensus around this is emerging as the cost/benefit analysis has moved decidedly in the direction of benefit. A long standing moralizing policy that creates even worse problems is a piece of ideologizing mischief that any Middle Way would set aside.

The emerging Colorado initiative is a decisive first salvo against the wall of hypocrisy and corruption that is the policy of criminalization. A first state domino is falling with many to follow with probably Federal recognition being the last to fall.

Long standing bad policy with an entrenched constituency is a hard nut to crack.

An inherent responsibility of the Federal government is the overseeing of the regulation of the economy. Various institutions contribute to this effort. Before proceeding to specific detail, an historical and sociological comment is in order. Free society is possible only on the basis of work.

> At the base of this democracy (Ancient Greece) and this culture lies the production and distribution of wealth. Some men can govern states, seek truth, make music, carve statues, paint pictures, write books, teach children, or serve the gods because others toil to grow food, weave clothing, build dwellings, mine the earth, make useful things, transport goods, exchange them, or finance their production or their movement. Everywhere this is the foundation. [37]

Through the ages the issues remain the same. It is only through productive work that sufficient goods and services are produced and distributed for the well being of all. Through productive work a person achieves a self-respect that entitles him to the esteem of those around him. Equally, it is through work that one can better oneself and then enjoy the resulting rewards. Work is the fundamental defining criterion of modern industrial society. It has proportionate rewards for those who do *all that they can*, those who do *less than they can*, and those who *do nothing at all*. Not to work is to invite the vices of excessive empty time. Alcohol and drug use and related criminal activity finds its primary cause in the effort to *kill time*, in the tedious effort to get through the boredom of yet another day of nothing.

Furthermore, the activities of doing nothing impose a penalty on productive work. Not to work is to incur a social cost that with each passing year has become more and more difficult to pay. As is obvious, many social problems begin in the idle of unemployment.

The Federal government would adopt a policy of full employment. Surprisingly, this has never been the stated objective of the United States, presumably the government "of the people." In the ever-vigilant fight against inflation, the central economic tool at the Federal Reserve Board has been to *increase unemployment*. When prices move upward, interest rates are raised by the Fed causing a higher cost for doing business. This higher interest cost "cools" the economy by causing a recession. Business activity is less, capacity reduced, and unemployment increased. Upward wage pressures are lessened as the pool of workers without jobs increases. Higher wages though are but one of the elements of inflation, among others that include higher health care costs, higher resource costs, and higher cartel managed energy costs. But the Fed's fight against inflation is directed predominantly at the wage element of the equation. In other words, the social misery of the unemployed and underemployed is deemed the appropriate cost for a democratic society to pay in order to limit inflation. So as not to erode the purchasing power of the wealthier citizens, those who are the least able are called upon to make a total sacrifice. The newly mustered unemployed are the Fed's "foot soldiers" in its battle to secure the economic well being of others. Fed policy takes from the givers and gives to the takers. The Fed overlooks the social cost of its monetary policy and simply imposes its "economic model." One sector of society pays dearly for the compounded comfort of another. The Fed's rightful mission is to manage the value of money and the raising of interest rates is one of its legitimate tools, but its fight against inflation extracts a very high social cost. Fed policy has simply been too extreme in targeting one factor of the economic equation for the total cost of inflation control. Computer related productivity gains have created a new economic model where full employment and increasing productivity does not result in higher inflation. This shift of paradigm needs to be more fully appreciated by the generally "backward looking" Fed. More recent Fed policy has recognized the legitimate goal of reduced unemployment but under a possible NUA jurisdiction that goal would stand at the forefront. High levels of employment create the demand that powers the economy more fully and extends heightened prosperity to both the middle class and corporate owners, or, simply, there is achieved *benefit for all.*

Another related issue concerns America at its deepest level and involves its image of itself as it goes about the world. It concerns the nature of international trade and the balance of power.

As the United States came to global prominence following World War II it reversed its policy on trade from one of protectionism to what has come to be called "free trade." As countries were lined up in the grand strategy for the defense of the Free World, the many separate national economies were forced to play by the new rules of development, which meant open markets. Small closed markets were opened to the force and presence of American business. The result was predictable. The small got smaller and weaker and the big got bigger and stronger. This new system of trade proved to have little about it that was free. There was a key exception to this development where a domestic market was never opened and instead was able to export unilaterally. Japan sells dramatically more cars in the United States then it buys. The Americans in their nearsighted and delusionary "wisdom" have allowed their own very important car market to be penetrated to an extent that extracts a huge domestic price. The way in which the "free trade" ideology was allowed to unfold has left a gigantic disparity between two of the world's largest trading partners. The Cold War implementation of the free trade ideology has allowed a closed market to remain closed as it in turn exports into an open market to its exclusive and unilateral advantage. The one refuses to buy in return and the other is left only buying. A fundamental imbalance has occurred that spells long-term economic disaster. The ideology of free trade has to be squared with the necessity for "fair trade." But the Americans persist in their heartfelt vision of the world that may ultimately leave them the loser.

Japan has a problem though that it cannot square with free trade. American foods, primarily rice, could be sold in Japan far cheaper than that produced by Japanese farmers, in fact these farmers simply could not compete and would be bankrupted. But, more is involved than just the cost of food commodities, as Japanese culture and traditions are held together by the landownership of these farmers. Simply, to open its rice market to American imports would destroy its own agriculture and much of its cultural heritage. More importantly, this would put the Japanese into the vulnerable position of being a possible economic hostage, something that no country can be expected to do. Certainly Americans would never tolerate this if conditions were reversed. A higher cost for rice has been deemed by the Japanese as the proper price to pay for retaining its own culture. Each country as a sovereign state must be allowed to protect what it sees as its fundamental rights. Yet, while the Japanese can protect their own markets as they see fit, the Americans need not continue to allow huge imports. The free trader's ideology collapses into wishful thinking when there is no reciprocity and with Japan there has been little. Talks of course are on-going, and the longer there is talk the more fully entrenched will become Japan's market share in the United States.

The French farmer is also under attack by the global free trader. The natural limitations of French farmers cannot compete against American "agribusiness" that produces on an immense scale. When the less efficient market is opened then its farmers will fail. It's predictable. "Cheap wheat" for the consumer will not be nearly as cheap when the social costs of a destroyed French agriculture are factored in. The concept of free trade is a "mathematical model" that has been conceived in isolation from the real world. It thinks of consumers, producers, prices, and markets as purely mathematical functions that can exist best in the "ivory towers" of its disciples. Yet *it serves as the justification for moral judgment.* More costly producers, such as Japanese rice farmers and French wheat farmers, are naturally less efficient and therefore "bad" and rightfully put out of business. If you are not the low cost producer, then you *ought* to be liquidated regardless of the fact that the natural order of one's society is undermined and great devastation visited upon the land. The free trader stands firm though, as it is cheaper and cheaper products for himself that he desires at whatever cost to others. In order that the more efficient American farmer may sell more of his product the Japanese and French farmers are permanently put off the land. Not everyone would think that this is a good thing.

The many proponents of free trade themselves will never suffer the effects of their theory as it is the quickly unseen and permanently unemployed who will suffer this misery. The free traders feel sanctioned to devastate the lives of others. Academic tenure and the high discretionary income of free trade think tankers and politicians protect them from sharing the fate of those that they have impoverished. Two issues are central here. Each country must be allowed to protect its own domestic market and balance its trade with all others. Japanese trade imbalances cannot be allowed to continue and American intrusion into the Japanese rice market cannot be imposed. Each country must be able to protect itself and then export to the level of its imports. Of course, international trade would continue at high levels but each market would have the right to choose whatever it sees as being best for itself. The Japanese and the French must be allowed the right to protect their farmers if they so choose. Ironically, the interests of American farmers are securely protected by import restrictions. Universal free trade is not a formula that can be forced on the world for mutual benefit. It's a prescription for big winners and equally big losers.

The issue of free trade needs to be looked at more closely. "Belief in free trade is as common and widespread among economists as belief in God is among clerics of less worldly religions." [38] Some background is in order.

> The United States had long ago called for a reduction of barriers to trade and investment throughout the world, on the grounds that humanity at large would benefit if individual producers were free to concentrate on what they could most efficiently produce. Indeed, Americans went farther than that. Wars, they tended to believe, grew out of rivalries resulting from economic nationalism; if nations could become economically interdependent, war itself might become obsolete. (Never mind that their own tariffs remained high throughout most of their history, or that the connection between trade, investment, and economic development was less than clear, or that the historical record suggested little correlation between extensive economic interchange and the avoidance of war.) And, yet, as had often been pointed out, the doctrine of 'free' trade brings disproportionate benefits to the most efficient producer, and the United States happened to find itself in that fortunate position throughout most of the twentieth century. Americans' disinterested endorsement of the 'open door,' therefore, served their self-interested ambition to expand markets, investment opportunities, and profits. [39]

A hypocrisy and deception stands at the center of the free trader's assumptions. While the term "free trade" may give the impression that it must involve equality, freedom, and the benefit of all, in fact, it involves absolute inequality, increasing dependence for most, and benefit to only a few. Those who have historically preached the gospel of free trade have been the English in the 18th century and the Americans after World War II. Each was then at the height of its economic dominance of the rest of the world. Each sought to use its privileged position to re-make the world in its own image, advantage, and profit. Free trade brings to the dominant producer the advantage of cheap materials and easy markets for its surplus. Both of these advantages of course are absolute. A dependent economy will never develop its own productive capacity if a stronger economy sells cheaply in its market. In effect, the weaker will always remain weaker and finally become merely a "plantation" in someone else's scheme of world order. This may all finally end in a new economic "colonialism." But an irony of sorts has become evident. America now has characteristics of both the dominant player and the plantation backwater. It hopes to sell to its own advantage and yet allows itself to be devastated by foreign exporters.

While the United States was opening markets in the wake of World War II, its newly acquired taste for global political dominance involved *giving away* its own market as a reward for those who were willing to line up on its side in its "defense of the free world." Simply, America gave away its economic advantage in order to stride atop the world as it saw fit. Countries were allowed special access to the American economy to the disadvantage of domestic producers and many succumbed to bankruptcy. Ironically, in a world of free traders, *America may lose.* The proverbial goose is now being cooked. The consequences of this have been that American workers have been idled and downgraded by the millions. None of this need continue. America may be weaker but it is still strong enough to regain its prosperity if it were but to choose to do so. National politicians often proudly talk of their "job creation" efforts, but the results are more a matter of downgrading, of the loss of a high paying job that affords a living and the gain of a low paying job that does not.

Free trade ideology cannot demand compliance. Export driven producer markets simply will not open themselves to foreign goods. It would be economic suicide. Whatever they may say and agree to today will have nothing to do with what they will do tomorrow. It is not so much a matter of dishonesty as it is a playing along with the insistent Americans who so fervently want to re-make the world. One thing is certain though, when all of this comes to grief the one commodity that will be freely traded will be accusation and blame.

> We have been told for years to bow down before
> "the market." We have placed our faith in the laws
> of supply and demand. What has been forgotten, or
> ignored, is that the market rewards only efficiency.
> Every other human value gets in the way. The
> market will drive wages down like water, until they
> reach the lowest level . . . Left to its own devices,
> the free market always seeks a work force that is
> hungry, desperate, and cheap—a work force that is
> anything but free.[40]

Environmental protection and cleanup would be enhanced. The obvious principle is the priority of the long-over the short-term. Environmental devastation will be visited upon the land after the *accumulation* of years of doing little or nothing. Action must be taken *now* to forestall and avoid this possible global demise that will be for everyone and everything equally. A Carbon Tax would be levied that would encourage and nurture the development and use of alternative fuels and technologies. Through taxation, the cost of carbon-based fuels would gradually rise. Much could be done that now simply lacks cost viability. The range of environmental policy can be easily visualized, being simply conservation, cleanup, and care. Many things could be done that would facilitate a policy of conservation. A few examples among a vast array will suffice. The toll road systems throughout the country create unnecessary pollution and congestion. Gasoline consumption while idling in line to pay a toll is a direct waste and without reasonable justification. If this toll system were to be dismantled, there would be both a reduction in pollution but also a greater efficiency of travel in urban areas that are near the limit of concrete gridlock. The "tolls" would be collected much more efficiently at the gasoline pump rather than every few miles on the road. Another example of easy conservation is reducible to a billboard type adage. "Cut less grass less often." It is simply wasteful to manicure thousands of acres of corporate grounds and homeowner lawns. Minor gasoline savings would be made but it would be part of a national program to encourage the "green" attitude. Hundreds, and even thousands, of energy conserving things mean little or nothing by themselves but when added together a great difference could be made. Most people would choose to do the right thing but find their single efforts to be meaningless. The missing catalyst is coherent national policy and committed leadership. Recognizing the added cost would convince many to think more of the advantages of consuming less.

> When we talk about energy conservation, we mean not just using *less* energy, but using energy more efficiently—that is, squeezing more work, more goods and services, more wealth from each kilowatt-hour we consume. In this sense, conservation is less a question of morals or ethics than of sound business practices: maximizing the profit we can make for each dollar we spend on energy. [41]

Of fundamental concern is energy policy. Partisan bickering and special interest positioning over an effort to raise the gasoline tax by 4 cents showcased poor policy and worse behavior. The purpose of a broad based Carbon Tax is not simply to raise revenue but, most importantly, to *encourage conservation* and facilitate the transition to alternative fuels and energy sources. The squabble had nothing to say about these benefits and hawked simply the pros and cons of a higher gas tax with respect to the various special interests. In the long term, the move to conservation and alternative energy sources is absolutely crucial. An additional $1 per gallon tax on carbon fuels, phased in possibly at $.02 per month would create incentives to conserve and disincentives to consume. A tax of this nature and magnitude would make competitive with carbon many very productive and promising technologies that now cannot compete with its artificially low price. "By making basic improvements to cars and buildings, America could save the energy equivalent of twelve million barrels of oil a day . . ." [42] The extensive network of carbon based special interests need to be convinced that they are welcome to be part of this transition and that their participation in this move to efficient energy policy is in their common interest. A world laid barren is a disaster for all. The oil companies, which would be expected to resist, ought to see that they are not merely in the oil business but rather in the much larger *energy* business.

> A carbon tax would rectify the myriad perverse incentives that today not only encourage wasteful building, driving, and other inefficiencies, but also give hydrocarbons an advantage over other energy technologies, such as hydrogen or renewables. [43]

A broadened perspective will allow oil companies to see profits far beyond the sale of oil, in fact they are perfectly positioned to take the greatest advantage of the necessary move to an energy system other than that of carbon. Furthermore, when calculating costs, such things as the Bush/Hussein War I and Bush/Hussein War II, are not included. Cheap oil is government policy but it is not necessarily as cheap as it seems. The dead and maimed of these wars bear witness.

The recent discovery of large pools of *additional* oil reserves cannot be taken as justification for the continuation of the oil consumption *status quo*. Long term it remains essential to diversify into technologies and methods that would greatly magnify the energy markets. "More for less" is the mantra that will serve the global common good. Rather than having a handful of possibilities it is necessary to pursue a thousand.

Another factor is important. The greatest fear of the totalitarian regime in Saudi Arabia is energy conservation in the United States. Ever increasing worldwide oil demand, led by huge American consumption, is the central element in the Saudi effort to prop up oil prices to a higher than real market level. (Some Texans may find a greater common interest with the Saudis than with their fellow Americans.) The United States' policy of deferring to this in order to prop up its own domestic oil market leads to inadequate efforts to conserve and reduce consumption. The Saudi policy that for the last 40 years has punished so severely the American economy is supported by American oil special interests. The Saudis of course are quite pleased. A conflict arises though for American society as a whole. By not conserving, the Saudi price for oil is paid by the American consumer, monies that then support huge building projects in Saudi Arabia, a monarchy whose second greatest fear is its own people. Some of this money of course gets re-directed to the funding of anti-Western terror. By not conserving, the American consumer is depleting the ability of the domestic economy to sustain itself and provide a high standard of living. The funding of foreign enemies is the unintended consequence of consumption driven energy.

A $1.00 per gallon additional Carbon Tax on petroleum would help to reverse this. A higher tax would encourage less consumption, thus reducing imported oil. In scrambling to replace lost revenues, overextended oil producers would increase production and compete with each other for a shrinking market and OPEC would dissolve. The producers would effectively lose control over prices. Oil prices would drop dramatically worldwide. Fewer dollars would flow out of the American economy. The real price of oil would drop but the additional $1.00 per gallon tax would be paid to the United States' treasury instead of into the King's purse. By conserving and taxing itself, monies would remain in the American economy for its own benefit. The net effect is in the common interest. The real price of oil would be less worldwide, aiding struggling economies everywhere, which often end up seeking American money to make up for their shortfalls. Alternatives to petroleum energy would be encouraged and a new generation of energy saving devices brought to the market. Monies would be kept in the United States to fund American prosperity instead of building palace cities in the sands of oil rich tyrannies of Arabia. Finally, the gross aggregate of petroleum-based pollution would be less. All of this for $1.00 per gallon, a bargain indeed. Most significantly, the American mentality towards energy would be transformed. Consuming less would come to be a personal responsibility as each person understands one's necessary contribution to the success of all. It would be something similar to the Homefront effort in World War II where people worked together to achieve more with less and were quite proud in having done so.

With systematic energy conservation in the United States the Saudis and the rest of their freeloading OPEC brethren and their few well connected friends in Texas would need to scramble against each other for the privilege of selling oil to the West for significantly less. Huge sums are now handed over to those who contribute *nothing* to global prosperity. Instead they use the threat of the constriction of supply in order to dole out domestic scarcity so as to maintain power as the few of the monarchy live in pure unearned abundance and then do everything in their considerable power to undercut the West's attempt to create an abundance that would serve the vastly greater general interest.

Of course, there is nothing special about this tax at the convenient number of $1.00 per gallon. What is crucial is that oil be taxed to the point where incentives for change take effect, where various alternative energy technologies become competitive, and then the necessary behavioral changes brought into play. The tax could be more or less, but at whatever rate, everyone with a stake in the American economy would be a grateful beneficiary.

Summarily, American energy policy is confused, near-sighted, and self-serving to a few vested interests.

> In practice, American energy policy is incoherent and fragmented, without anything resembling a long-term strategy. In writing energy legislation, American lawmakers tend to be parochial, as interested in rewarding, or punishing, various states, regions, or industries, as in advancing some overarching national energy strategy. The resulting energy laws are frequently wish lists aimed at protecting regional interests, such as those of oil producers in Texas or Alaska or coal-mining companies in the East and in Wyoming or the big utilities in the Midwest and South, or ethanol producers in the Corn Belt, or political interests of a particular lawmaker or committee chairperson. [44]

A perfect metaphor is perhaps possible. We, as a Nation, have a choice, a fundamental choice. It is a fact that the energy possibilities of the next 50 years will be dramatically different than has been the energy reality of the last 50 years. Great change is coming upon us, quickly. We can either load up our SUV and drive full speed over a cliff and hope for a soft landing when of course there will be none, or we can drive the imminently possible electric/gas hybrid car more slowly down a gently inclining slope. Only a blind, stupid, and bull-headed buffoon would choose the launching of the SUV into their grandchildren's world, yet to date that is the clear choice of American energy policy.

Environmental policy could be best summarized by the words of the renowned English fisherman Izaak Walton. "To strive for the purity of water, the clarity of air, and the wise stewardship of the land and its resources; to know the beauty and understanding of nature, and the value of wildlife, woodlands and open space; to the preservation of this heritage and to man's sharing in it." Regardless of the contested pros and cons concerning the issue of global warming, the enhancement of environmental conservation is the right policy.

Chapter Five
Budget and Taxation

The broadly diversified strength of the American economy enhances the possibility of a shift to the principles of the NUA. Taxation is central and with it there is to be encountered the howl of special interests and, like hungry wolves, they naturally abuse each other to get at the rapidly consumed carcass. Every partial theory of self-interest, masquerading as the common good, is to be found and it will be to the most ruthless that the spoils will go. The principle of taxation for the NUA will be to seek a balance and fairness among the competing sectors and will hinge most essentially upon a combination of reducing income taxes and increasing consumption taxes. Fashionable theory gives overriding advantage to the rich, with distorting and impoverishing consequences for the poor and middle class, but this must be questioned in its entirety.

The overriding first principle is that the U.S. Government has *the right to collect taxes*. This is not "theft" as some would claim. "In the absence of a legal system supported by taxes, there couldn't be money, banks, corporations, stock exchanges, patents, or a modern market—none of the institutions that make possible the existence of almost all contemporary forms of income and wealth." [45] It is only because of governmental institutions, the whole structure of civil society, that anyone is able to earn anything at all. Only on the basis of civil society is economic activity for the first time possible and therefore such institutions must be paid for first. Thereafter issues of taxation decide the question as to what a society chooses to be. The question here is quite simple. Does society choose to be more or less equal?

The ideological obsession with Supply Side economics must be understood as the electioneering fraud that it is. This modern equivalent of the Divine Right of Kings that is "all to the One" or, in this version, "all to the Few," has achieved an "iconic" status among some ideologues, who covet the power of elected office. This "voodoo economics" finally must be recognized as the hocus pocus that it is. The notion of giving to the rich by reducing their taxes does not bestow any "trickle down" benefits or blessings to everybody else at all. But the easily deluded proclaim the virtues of their self-interest *as if* that were the common good itself, but *it is not*.

> Reducing tax burdens for the wealth holders is a
> political program that will reward some citizens and
> penalize others. As an economic program, it does
> not yield the increased savings and investment and
> faster economic growth that the conservative logic
> promises. This is not entirely a secret. Conservative
> economists have pored over the numbers for years,
> searching for evidence to confirm their conviction
> that taxing the wealthy lightly benefits everyone
> else. In theory, they are sure it is right. Only they
> can't find much in the way of facts. [46]

The tax savings of the rich that are to be re-invested with the intention of powering the economy to better and better jobs for everyone else do nothing of the sort and instead these savings are pocketed for purposes of greater personal consumption. The general advantages that were to be created are converted instead into the particular pleasures of personal leisure. The Supply Side "solution" is no solution at all but rather an aggravating cause of the continuing problem. Increasing the supply of goods to those who can ill-afford anything at all in the first place would not generate general prosperity but would create only unsold inventories.

> In other words, Mellon (a major proponent)
> had it backwards and so do later generations of
> his apostles. A growing economy with widely
> distributed incomes and full employment creates
> the effective demand that leads investors to increase
> capital investment—new factories and more jobs.
> Capital will not build new factories to make goods
> that no one can afford to buy. [47]

The few wealthy cannot create sufficient general demand, something that is possible only by meeting the needs of the many that are not wealthy. It is not on the Supply Side but on the *Demand Side* that general prosperity will be achieved. ". . . the trickle-down theory is not empirically confirmed." [48] "There are those who believe that, if you will only legislate to make the well-to-do prosperous, their prosperity will leak through on those below. The Democratic idea, however, has been that if you legislate to make the masses prosperous, their prosperity will find its way up through every class which rest above them." [49] "Trickle-down economics was never much more than just a belief, an article of faith." [50] The statistical reality of trickle-down voids the theory.

> The numbers are stark. The top 1 percent pocketed
> 42 percent of the stock Market gains between
> 1989 and 1997, while the top 10 percent of the

population took 86 percent. "There was almost
no trickle-down of growth to the average family.
Almost all the growth in household income and
wealth has accrued to the richest twenty percent." [51]

Trickle-down is a ruse for a "gush-up" that the wealthy will take straight to the bank after having written a considerable check to the architects of their unnecessary but welcome windfall. The religion is without sanction, even though the High Priests continue without pause to preach the salvation of the faith and then driving the National Debt to new levels of the incomprehensible. This ideology continues to confuse and twist economic policy but now needs to be set aside. But something more is at issue. It concerns the psychology of power.

While the possession of sufficient money and then wealth, allows one no longer to experience the anxiety of possible scarcity, having "stockpiled," as it were, it also allows for a real power over those who are without. The experience of the rich is at its most satisfying when it involves a power to determine the conditions of those that are necessarily under their dominion. It is a great satisfaction to draw the distinction between one's own life of leisure and that of one's workers. It is the difference between finding every door open to one's touch and finding no doors at all, between relaxing at ease and working under duress. It is the difference between the privilege of access and the fact of none at all. This difference lends style and class to a life of leisure that is obviously distinct from the noisy hubbub of everyone else. Simply, the rich take great pride in being who they are and expect respectful recognition and acknowledgment from everyone else. The pillars that hold up the ideology of privilege find expression in Supply Side economics and the exquisite experience of privilege and condescension itself. When one has the power to treat all others as servants one ought to be entitled to their quiet servitude.

A brief comment regarding greed is possible. A simple definition will do. Greed is the taking from someone else that then will go without while one has more than could possibly be needed. Greed is corporations which under fund their agreed upon pensions yet over fund executive pay. Greed is an employer taking all the credit and giving all the blame in order to justify a restriction in wages. Greed is the Federal Reserve Board unemploying millions in order to protect the wealthy from modest inflation. Greed is corporations moving "offshore" in order to boost profits at the expense of the unemployed. Greed is corporate "raiders" dismantling productive organizations in order to sell the pieces for an immediate profit and someone else's debt. Greed is the demolition of companies in order to raid pension funds. Workers, the givers, can "go to hell" as free market capitalism rages throughout the land. Greed is the act of intentionally making someone else's life worse simply for the sake of it or, as is often done, simply for the *sport* of it. And greed, finally, is being in the privileged position to be a positive force in the world and choosing instead the greater personal profits to be made from asserting the purely negative. In a word, it is selfishness. In a world that is shared by all, this imposes a liability that is more and more difficult to sustain. The Ancient Greeks understood this well.

> Show me the man who asks an over-abundant share
> of life, in love with more, and ill content with less,
> and I will show you one in love with foolishness. In
> accumulation of many years pain is in plenty, and
> joy not anywhere when life is over-spent. [52]

Or, elsewhere. "One part of our ills comes from the fact that too many men are shamefully rich and too many desperately poor." [53] When the middle class comes under attack, when its health and prosperity is sacrificed to the rich or the poor, then the great engine of economic growth is undercut and diminished and finally no longer an engine at all.

Something has emerged which has fundamentally altered the terms of the equation between the rich and the rest, between privilege and daily labor. The economic base has expanded to the point where there now may be *enough to go around*. This stunning accomplishment raises the prospect of no longer needing to covet beyond possible need. As the tax code is written and re-written, this fact is not considered, as the old assumptions continue with new ferocity in the face of better evidence to the contrary. Various commentators, intent upon emotional titillation and hysteria, reduce the issue to the single aspect of taxation. Everything else is made to ride on this one issue. What is lost of course is the entire context of social life, the relationship between expectation and reality, between social costs and benefits, between human beings and other human beings living in the same world. What is lost is the notion of *balance* in the play of equally valid concerns. What is lost is simple respect for one's fellow human being. A tax policy could be enacted that would strive to establish that missing respect to the benefit of all. Simply, it is not the amount of tax that one pays that is important, but rather the quality of one's life that remains after having paid one's rightful share. What is important is the standard of living that one's retained income will sustain with respect to the world as a whole. Ironically, those with the very highest standard of living in the history of the world clamor the very loudest for "tax relief" as without it they proclaim the "end of the world." Nowhere is there greater self-righteous exaggeration than with issues where the comfortably well off demand yet more at the cost of all others.

The income tax structure would be greatly reduced and a National Sales Tax put into place. The "pork barrel" trough of deductions would be done away with. Elections are won and lost with the promises of special "targeted tax cuts" through the maze of special interest deductions. This virtual "race to the bottom" would be put to rest. Privileged power would no longer so easily take simply to itself. A inclusive National Sales Tax would be infinitely easier to collect and would be paid by everyone proportionate to their individual consumption. Taxpayers would determine their own rate of taxation based upon their freely chosen level of consumption. Consume more, pay more. Consume less, pay less. A re-positioning would occur, where income taxes are now collected as a sales tax. The individual levy would be nearly the same as a broader fairness is enacted. The point then is not to raise overall taxes but rather to shift the source of their collection so that positive behavior is encouraged and the opportunity for political special interest "pork" reduced. A National Sales Tax of perhaps 6% would be a clear and fair way in which to collect revenue. Great degradation to the American political body occurs when the voracious special interests are fed at the expense of general integrity, when the "political process" is reduced simply to the daily task of this feeding. An exception would be made for above average earners where a reasonable flat tax would be levied. The privilege accorded to those at the top ought to be taxable in an appropriate way.

A relatively efficient and fair tax could be levied at the very heart of American Capitalism. A Financial Transaction Tax would be collected on the sale of equity assets. This would be relatively easy to collect, fairly extended across the economy, and encouraging of long-term investment rather than short-term speculation. Volatility would be reduced in the market and the speculators replaced by investors.

In general, then, the principle of greater tax fairness would be implemented, expanding the tax base so as to reduce the liability for any given individual. People would profit through business initiatives rather than through the manipulation of tax laws and financial deal making. Real economic productivity rather than financial sleights of hand would produce wealth. Too many take for themselves in the name of an "economic theory" that simply shifts the burden to the unprivileged majority.

An essential definition of a restructured tax code would be to move in the direction of efficient *collectability*. Tax loopholes have been put into place by those special interests with sufficient power to impose a minority advantage at the expense of the majority. Operating within a system of self-serving "smoke and mirrors" the few pay less or very little as the rest pay more or simply the shortfall is added to the Federal debt. Broad based and comprehensive sales taxes as a partial substitute for income taxes would eliminate special interest advantage and greatly facilitate legitimate collection. Many rue the continued accumulation of debt yet laud the avoidance of rightful taxation. Are we sophisticated hypocrites or just simple fools?

As the status of the American military is the essential issue with respect to International Relations, and the transformation of health care is the essential issue for Social Relations, so it is that the issue of Social Security and Medicare is essential for issues with respect to Budget and Taxation. It is with this though that the NUA principles of responsibility, the long term, and the common interest are perfectly in place and could inform policy most effectively. Current recipients are entangled in a hypocrisy, which their self-interest refuses to acknowledge. The generation that won World War II came home to experience the greatest economic expansion in history. Continents devastated by war were the necessary condition of this prosperity. An escalation in real wages and real estate values created new wealth. Simply, this generation will go down in history as the most privileged. It is unlikely that any other will ever experience such a profound accumulation of wealth. Wages paced ahead of inflation and significant capital gains were returned on the sale of two or more homes. Equally significant, as this group aged they became a dominant political force. Age votes, youth does not. In appealing to this voting bloc, politicians continued to promise and deliver increasingly generous benefits that were beyond legitimate actuarial projections. They were getting far more than their contribution could justify. An enormous special interest was constituted that could dictate its own terms. In a budgetary climate of lesser competitors, the grandparents will always win. But the win is hollow, as it is bankrupting the next generations. Without any central consensus each group gets what it can and then these privileges are wrapped in the romance of entitlement. But the contradiction now becomes evident.

The single greatest looming catastrophe facing the nation is the ballooning retirement of the baby boomers, the sons and daughters of the World War II generation, who will draw from Social Security and Medicare entitlements in an amount that is beyond all comprehension. One estimate claims that the *shortfall* for this group, the amount not to be collected, is *$45 trillion.* [54]

> There is, however, one serious problem with these figures, not with the calculations that underlie them but with their *acceptance*. To put it bluntly, this news is so bad that scarcely anyone believes it. It is not that people are completely oblivious of the problem. It is common knowledge that Americans are living longer and that paying for the rising proportion of elderly people in the population is going to be expensive. What people do not realize is just how expensive. [55]

The most affluent generation that cherishes its grandchildren has *deeded a national debt* in their name that is simply unpayable. A generation that may be the luckiest in history has chosen to bequeath to its heirs a lesser world simply to maintain a retirement that refuses to accept a more rightful share. This is the height of irresponsibility by those who know better. But their lobbyists chant and chatter and prior to the final collapse "all is well." But it is clear that the excesses of the grandparents will be visited upon the children and grandchildren. This need not be the case. A political realignment towards the consensus of the middle would be able to address these issues without bombast and exaggeration and the majority would recognize that enough is enough and that some re-definition in benefits is both possible and necessary. They would also understand that this is something that should be done and the proper vote ought to be cast. They would choose to end the hypocrisy and finally square their care for their grandchildren with the world that will remain with their passing. A means-test would be implemented where only those without sufficient means for retirement would receive benefits. Those comfortably well-off, those who have benefited the most from the economic system, would no longer be entitled to a monthly Social Security payment. Only those in legitimate need would be paid. No one would suffer from such a change. In the context of diminishing resources few things could be more painless. Not to make such a relatively easy change would signal that no change anywhere would be allowed. We would have chosen to be happy with doing nothing to save ourselves. This money saved and then re-positioned has an infinitely greater value when re-allocated for the common good rather than being dispersed for individual consumption. The benefits of those truly in need would be maintained. A generation of people that has profited so handsomely from an economic system of unprecedented prosperity may *choose* to give back for the general benefit of all.

A general economic principle needs to be re-stated. It is not on the Supply-Side but rather on the Demand-Side that general prosperity occurs. On the Demand-Side there is broad based democratic participation rather than the Supply-side call for cartel-like centralization. A whole list of problems can be more rationally addressed from the Demand-Side. Whether it is health care, the Drug War, energy policy, or tax policy, it is on the Demand-Side that progress is to be made. The Supply-Side drives to reinforce existing difficulties to the immediate profit of its selected constituencies. It is the aggregate choices of general participation and not the narrow self-interests of a few that will afford the opportunities for everyone to do better.

With the totality of budgetary and taxation changes that are embodied in the NUA one is left with *a balanced budget*. The net effect of all policy changes is a tendency towards a balance between spending and taxation. It is the "dirty" politics of targeted deductions and credits and failed economic theory that has driven the budget into vast arrears. To be oblivious to the obvious can no longer pass as acceptable policy. Accumulated debt consumes like a cancer, accelerating to a reckoning that all would agree would be none too nice. A return to the Middle Ages would be significantly demeaning to most everyone.

An ideological judgment regarding the NUA agenda could assert that it is not a center position at all but rather essentially motivated by "Leftist" tendencies, after all any policy that takes inspiration from the *Demand-Side* is necessarily to the Left of Center. Yes, in a way, but it is all retrieved to the middle by the fundamental fact that all of this resides within the domain of the individual. For example, the central wellspring of any National Health Plan is the contribution made by the person as a matter of human agency, so that the "Leftist" single payer system is squared at the center by the "Rightist" deference to individual choice. With the rightful perspective a balance is achieved where any drive to extremism is left wanting. As with this then, so with the rest of the NUA political philosophy and agenda, there is individual responsibility only within the context of social responsibility.

Chapter Six
Semi-Universal Basic Income

Whether animal, plant, or matters of human cultural activity, there is always an evident pattern. Things of all sorts are born, grow, mature, and in turn decline into something else. Obvious enough. Each individual phase of this living process is marked by a uniquely appropriate methodology. An intrinsic continuity emerges that is subject to fundamental transformation. Supersession occurs where the earlier gives way to the later as each coalesces to establish ever renewing conditions. At issue are simply the successive stages of life, be that biological or cultural. A plant, for example, beginning as the seed that has been cast off from the prior year's "parent," emerges in an initial growth where all efforts are put to the growth itself until there is achieved a maturity that is able to flourish as the forces of reproduction begin to take place. Having then accomplished its function it begins a decline and final death as the new year gives way and renewal can begin in a sort of indefinite recurrence of the same. All of this is quite obvious but with more unique examples this principle is more easily lost in the greater complexity that is naturally involved. Economic life, a most complex example, follows the same contours, as beginning, growth, maturity, and decline. Continuity and non-continuity work together ensuring the process forward. "Paradigm Shift" is the famous term for the transitions of one phase to the next.

It may be useful to consider the essential structure of capitalism and its possible conformity, or not, to the universal principle of beginning, growth, maintenance, and decline. This could be the foremost example of cultural accomplishment and achievement. When capitalism emerges from its conditions of beginning, to growth, to maintenance, and possible final decline, how does it shift from one paradigm to the next? What does the history of capitalism have to teach us?

The tentative answer to these questions obviously requires a return to the beginning. In primitive life the overwhelming experience is that of scarcity in all of its manifestations. There is very seldom enough to go around as only in perhaps the random times of a successful hunt when, around the campfire, all will get their fill. In the world of hunting and gathering the cycle of not enough and then enough grinds forward without end. In the medieval world of larger settlements and reliance on agriculture and animal domestication there remains the primary fact of there not being consistently enough. Occasional abundance may occur but it is easily hoarded and consumed by the overlord and his lieutenants as they become takers with no thought of the welfare for the rest, the many more givers. Political and economic power is reserved for the few as the notion of sharing is inconceivable. In this first instance of the Zero-Sum game, where one can win only if the other loses, there is little thought of "capital investment" where some limited surplus could be set aside for the bad times that will surely return. At some fortuitous time a change of circumstance presented itself as an alternative. Medieval production eked out a surplus that became a set aside that served as the basis of an investment that would compound into future profits. A seed would have been planted that suggested a future return. Initially, of course, this could be an opportunity for only a few as the vast majority of people would be worked to an early grave as laborers and soldiers. The common run of mankind would be used up, consumed, in the process of creating a greater investment opportunity. The newly minted capitalist needed to impose near-starvation wages in order to accumulate yet more capital. Religious and moral justification was invoked to assure the few that this was all very proper and in the name of God, socially expressed in the new theory of the "survival of the fittest," or Social Darwinism. The working masses needed to suffer and that was just the long and short of it, as others must command the "compounding profit." At a time of the *potential* for increasing abundance there would be no sense of an equitable sharing as newly mandated scarcity continued to grip the land. The seed of capitalism had given rise to the growth of accumulation as consolidated production begins to move forward. In a relatively short period of time a vast scientific, technological, and industrial infrastructure was put into place that would produce beyond any tentative ability to comprehend. In theory the new abundance would be reserved for the few. Notwithstanding, middle class life became possible as the newly shared profits needed to be invested more broadly. The seed that had become growth had now in turn achieved a stature that shifted effort to maintenance. In building this system that included manufacturing, agriculture, transportation, government, research and development, and education, all of which had been built by the "worker" who had come to be a willing and productive partner with the continuing powers of investment ownership. A massive system of global production has been created through the methods of capitalistic growth but the question arises as to whether those methods of growth remain appropriate to continued maintenance? Will what got us here take us any further? The natural assumption of course is a resounding yes, that the capitalism that created growth will sustain maintenance. But problems loom in unexpected ways. Long held assumptions can easily over time become questionable.

The uniquely stunning success of capitalism, creating a massive accumulation of wealth, evidenced by the totality of the industrial-technological edifice, sets the conditions for the possibility of its transformation into something more, something stunningly different. The power of growth could be superseded by the greater reality of maintenance. In having built the industrial-technological system there becomes less and less need to continue to build, as the total system achieves maturity. The edifice once built no longer needs builders. A workforce fully employed will give way to a diminished aggregate demand of required labor. This trajectory will be enhanced with the explosive power of technological innovation as productivity gains require less and less labor. Unemployability will skyrocket as millions will go without even the prospect of a livable job. Income Disparity is the catch-phrase that will define the developing imbalance. Profits though will equally skyrocket but only to the lucky few as super-abundance will be encircled by pervasive want. An unimaginable abundance will exist at the center of an unimaginable scarcity. The few will take shelter in personal fortresses as the many roam the countryside. Results would be predictable, civil war until the inevitable return to a new Stone Age, a fight to the finish where everybody loses.

Proponents of conservative economic theory embrace an affirmation of the virtues of the growth of capitalism. Looking to the record of this past success, it is assumed that more of the same is most logically appropriate. The methods of success just need to be continued, an assumption that may be subject to re-consideration. A New Capitalism based upon an accomplished general abundance would re-set the relationship between the individual and the social. The essential achievement will be attained when the one and the many mutually support one another rather than continuing with the well-worn struggle and animosity of the zero-sum game, where many more must lose for anyone to win. When all do better it is possible to find an economic well-being that is sustainable as win/win overcomes win/lose. A New Socialism is simply the notion that economic win/win is possible and inherently desirable and sustained by a transformed Old Capitalism. The maintenance of capitalism needs to be re-constituted with respect to the principles of its initial growth. This discussion could be specifically entertained with respect to the difference between Supply-side and Demand-side economics.

It is necessary to re-state this in terms that would give a more precise definition of this New Socialism. As one considers the state of the world and the general trends of the next 50 to 100 years there is much that is disturbing in a fundamental way. Heading the list of forthcoming troubles is the massive income disparity that so perfectly pits the rich against the rest as the rich hunker down in gated enclaves and the rest struggle to survive. The one lives in unfettered abundance while the other grapples with daily scarcity. In-between these polar extremes lay the middle class that is strung tighter and tighter as many more fall into poverty than rise into wealth. The mother of all problems, the mother giving birth to sundry offspring, then is income disparity, the single most profound driver of social division. If Old Capitalism is the engine of income disparity, then computer-enhanced automation is its fuel. More and more efficient production by fewer and fewer people is a zero-sum game that powers a race to the bottom. Amid pockets of unimaginable wealth, a fever of despair lays upon the land. Corporate profits stagger to ever higher levels of concentration as fewer and fewer workers are employed. Stock values surge when workforce levels plummet as the few cash-in and the many cash-out. Short-term self-interest, buttressed by political and economic ideologies of winner-take-all, lead to a social imbalance that sooner or later will deliver a comeuppance that will be nothing short of hell on earth. Income disparity is class war where all will be lost, a suicidal fight to the finish. With the power to dictate election results our "democracy" will be forsaken as money and power merge to give "victory" to the few. The New Oligarchy will mandate to its own advantage as it ironically enough doesn't see that the products which it produces in such abundance are no longer affordable by a vanishing middle-class consumer market. The goose is being cooked. The whole thing lets loose as a sort of initially slow moving mudslide that necessarily gathers speed and force melding into an avalanche that bears the earmarks of a tsunami that ends in a very large pile of mud at the bottom. The distinction between rich and poor will have been swept away as all are now equally dead. Any most unfortunate survivors will trudge aimlessly into a New Stone Age.

If income disparity pits the rich and the rest and is the essential core of the imbalance, then is there a proactive and reasonable way in which to mitigate the inevitable consequences and find a balance that *benefits both*? Recent and not so recent commentary centers on the concept of a *Universal Basic Income* (UBI), a monthly payment to everyone over 21 a minimum dollar amount that would be sufficient to cover the cost of a partial basic standard of living. Anyone earning less than $40,000 a yaer would qualify. This would just be a *start* that would lift people out of dire poverty as they would then work to go further. *Set an income floor that extends to millions an opportunity to do better.* Pay those qualified $800 per month. This infusion of cash would necessarily be spent and much good would ensue. The consumer economy would boom. A simple way forward exists then that would power this decrease in income disparity even further, having a greater economic impact, and costing half as much. Give the monthly payment to only the bottom half of per capita income, using a formula that factors in existing wealth, (income plus assets), thus the Semi being proposed. It is only the poorest that need this infusion as they would *immediately spend it.* Giving extra money to those who already have enough is not to spur new spending as instead it will be idled. The economic dynamic of Semi-Universal Basic Income (SUBI) is one of "trickle-up," not "trickle-down." Demand-side" not "Supply-side" is the economic model for dispensing the greater good. Everyone does better.

It is easy to imagine the howls of protest that would ensue from those on the top. Chain-privilege and self-serving Supply-siders would claim that this is nothing but socialism run amok and that the privileged top half has *earned* their way and it is work, not entitlement, that determines one's place in the world. This is but another attack on the rich, soak-em. Of course this is as true as it is false. Breaking down this proposal into its component parts it is possible to see that there is an equitable middle ground. Wealth has very little to do with work as any amount of work will never make you wealthy. Billionaires do not work for a living. Much of the accumulation of wealth has to do with luck, or the confluence of forces and circumstances that have nothing to do with the efforts of the possible beneficiary, the rich man. The realm of the *unearned* is vast and available to but a few, dictated by the "rules of the game," being the privileged remain privileged through generations. Inheritance is the primary road to wealth, if you can arrange it. Someone's death gives to someone else an unearned windfall. Inheritance comes in forms other than the strictly monetary. Being born into the already existing social and economic elites is a very good way to go. Privilege becomes habitual from childhood and it is easy to overlook the advantages that accrue and see their head-start as "the way God intended." Privilege will find many doors open on the way to more accumulating wealth as the vast majority of people will find no doors at all. The wealthy are not morally superior and the poor therefore morally inferior, as each has just been given a different draw in the game of life. More specifically, the realm of the unearned includes stock dividends, capital gains, stock buybacks, rents, gifts, corporate bonuses, stock manipulations by Wall Street, cartel pricing, etc. Wealth then is essentially unearned and necessarily on the backs of real wage earners. With SUBI the work ethic would not be undermined but rather enhanced as with a monthly payment *and* work a person could emerge out of poverty and stand to get ahead. Without the payment there is little chance of doing so. Once locked at the bottom, there is no exit.

Demand-side economics could be characterized as "direct infusion" to those in need. Supply-side "economics" is wishful thinking by those set to be the first beneficiaries. It is naked self-interest taken to the extreme of vicious self-aggrandizement, just "the way of world" but of course it is not. The irony is that the ensuing general economic boom with SUBI will return new profits to the owners of wealth, win-win. The Supply-side pits society against itself, a zero-sum game with few winners and many losers (pre-determined) while the Demand-side orchestrates mutual benefit to most everyone that chooses to participate. What is at issue is the fact that capitalism has achieved the historical threshold of its transformation from narrow wealth formation and concentration to an accelerated wealth formation and its equitable general sharing. A world of majority scarcity could be transformed into a world of general abundance to everyone's benefit. Rather than pitting individual against individual it is possible to envision a world of working together. Inclusion, not exclusion, would power the general economy forward as the high cost of poverty is converted into prosperity. The rich will howl in self-righteous indignation as if their "first born" would be sacrificed on the bonfires of a new socialism, as their hired lobbyists scurry to-and-fro but, upon careful consideration, it is evident that working together is far superior to working apart. Cooperation, not competition, is the essential accomplishment of "maintenance capitalism," as it is transformed from an ideology of "all for himself" to an efficient purveyor of general health and well-being. The traditional cost of social stress, criminality of all sorts, would be dramatically reduced and then off-setting some of the cost. How to pay? Any final numbers would be difficult to establish, but a "ballpark" figure is possible.

Consensus estimates of a SUBI range around 1 trillion dollars per year. New revenues would be necessary.

1) A Financial Transaction Tax (FTT) would be implemented as a 1% surcharge on all financial transactions.
2) An annual Wealth Tax on assets of $2 million to $10 million would be charged at a rate of 1%. Assets above $10 million would be charged 2%. Assets over $1 billion would be charged 3%.
3) Inheritance taxes would be implemented.
4) Carbon (gas) Tax of $.50 per gallon.
5) National Sales Tax (inclusive) of 5%.

Taxing those at the top does them no intrinsic harm but does much for those at the bottom. The Financial Transaction Tax will be fought tooth and nail by a Wall Street contingent that believes itself exempt from a legitimate and fair tax on the financial system. While the less affluent pay a sale tax on most things the well-heeled pay none on the buying and selling of financial assets. It's a tax that would be hardly noticed and would slow "day trading" volatility, an activity that contributes nothing of value. A Wealth Tax is perfectly obvious. Massive accumulations of wealth in the hands of so few could easily be re-allocated to where it would contribute much more value to the general economy. No one would go without. Inheritance represents the single greatest vehicle for the accumulation of un-earned income. Having been born into privilege as a random act of nature the generationally wealthy can easily contribute more. A Carbon Tax would tax everyone but since the lifestyle of the wealthy "burn much more gas" it would be an appropriate source of new revenue. Quit with the feeding of the special interests at the public trough where lobbyists fight among themselves with pre-determined winners and losers and instead extend to everyone the chance to do better. Any final numbers would be established in due course but this provides a general structure of possibility. Some few will take advantage of this policy of equitable distribution as is always the case but in general much good could possibly ensue. Financial help that is extended now would better ensure a more prosperous next generation. Saving kids from crippling poverty is a giant step forward for everyone. Moving money from the top to the bottom harms no one.

I am now convinced that the simplest approach will prove to be the most effective—the solution to poverty is to abolish it directly by a now widely discussed measure: the guaranteed income. The contemporary tendency in our society is to base our distribution on scarcity, which has vanished, and to compress our abundance into the overfed mouths of the middle and upper classes until they gag with superfluity. If democracy is to have breadth of meaning it is necessary to adjust this inequity. It is not only moral, but it is also intelligent. We are wasting and degrading human life by clinging to archaic thinking. Martin Luther King[56]

The basic idea is to use the mechanism by which we now collect tax revenue from people with incomes above some minimum level to provide financial assistance to people with incomes below that level. Milton Freidman.[57]

There is no reason why in a free society government should not assure to all, protection against severe deprivation in the form of an assured minimum income, or a floor below which nobody need descend. F.A. Hayek.[58]

In thinking through the philosophically possible one is well positioned to consider the specific details of the probable such that the actual emerges in the good faith effort to achieve the greater good. It is eternally one's choice to do one thing or another. Insight into possible long term consequences may tip one's choice to do the right thing for one's grandchildren.

As the Old Guard Conservative Supply-siders continue to die off and the newer Millennials achieve political maturity the electoral process will naturally move in the direction of Demand-side transformation. Moving on from an earlier version of capitalism, it may be possible to choose a more equitable way of living-together, without relinquishing the basic tenets of Old Capitalism. Things still have time to get much worse but that very fact may be the condition for the possibility of the transformation herein suggested. When the old "solutions" obviously and miserably fail, it perhaps becomes much easier to consider something radically different. The "way of the world" may again factor into this consideration. Old Capitalism assumes the first validity of the motivating value of competition, cut-throat at times, but always adding to the common good. The next generation New Capitalism is moving in a different direction as it is understood that lasting value is not in competition but rather in *cooperation*. The "Way of the World" is in the process of being re-constituted with respect to cooperation, as competition loses its appeal as a winner-take-all ideology. The over-accumulation of zero-sum relationships is being overtaken by the recognition of the possibility of equitable sharing and caring when there is obviously enough to go around, as abundance abounds.

The SUBI does not subvert capitalism rather it takes capitalism into a more mature dimension that solidifies an inclusive economic base. This is not the demolition of capitalism but rather its consummation as the engine of an equitable participation for all. Capitalism, as currently constituted, simply leaves too many people behind. The full power of capitalism can be invoked with its broader transformation. Those locked out of the system can be more readily included.

General theory must run into the particulars of specific consequences that then need to be evaluated with respect to long term possibilities. What would be the specific consequences of a re-constituted capitalism? What would be the general benefit of a shift from Supple-side to Demand-side capitalism?

- Structural poverty would be reduced.
- Criminal activity would be reduced.
- Judicial costs would be reduced.
- Incarceration costs would be reduced.
- Social strife would be reduced.
- The cost of the implementation of existing social programs would be reduced.
- Workforce participation would increase as the chronically desperate would at last see hopeful possibility.
- Unpaid labor would be paid such as home health care. Volunteer work of all kinds would be subsidized. People could more easily give of their time.
- Positive social harmony would be increased.
- General economic activity would be increased as all of the subsidy would need to be spent.
- Income disparity would be reduced yet the top would continue to receive increasing profits from the increase of consumer spending. Owning corporate America leaves the wealthy just as wealthy if not more so. Moving some tax dollars from the top to the bottom leaves everyone better off.

If nothing is done to alter the trajectory of existing economic and social policy there will be hell to pay as the newly enlisted army of the downtrodden will increase. Income disparity will continue to surge forward with increasing social devastation.

One could envision a civil war that would consummate the "greatest country" coming to a very ignoble end. Capitalism is in need of a fundamental transformation that looks to the future and acts to do better. The capitalistic ideology of the past will not carry us forward. It is to 2050 and beyond that we must look, not to 1890. It is not to Make America Great Again, a nostalgia of a mythical past, but rather a Make America Better, a look to the future, a Look to the Good, to which we need to turn our attention, so that everyone does better.

It is self-confidently and self-righteously claimed that this possible "handout" will produce nothing but moral degradation and supplement personal sloth, that one must *work* oneself forward. True enough in ideal circumstances such as in the founding of America when open possibility and expansion constituted the status quo but that nostalgic past no longer exists. Living wage jobs are being systematically eliminated, as more and more people are trapped at the bottom, living lives of quiet desperation and while the legend of "rags to riches" may apply to some few for the many more it is a cruel fiction. Everyone benefits from moving resources from the top to the bottom. In an electoral system this could be easily elected into place as demographically the bottom half far outnumbers the top half. The virtue of this is that it is not a narrowly "targeted" benefit, one directed to a politically important constituency that needs a specific boost for electoral purposes, but rather it provides general benefit to all those in need.

An easy and ready-made objection is that the SUBI would prompt massive fraud and corruption and that this "give-away" would flounder from its very nature. Certainly, some of this would be inherent as it is in any social program, the negative unintended consequences, but the net gain would far out-run the net loss. Even a 5% fraud rate could not diminish the value of a 95% gain. Many more children would eat better as some few would cheat the benefit. Exceptions never negate the rule but rather confirm that rule. It would not be any worse than the existing patchwork of numerous overlapping programs. Of course the program could be designed to limit any possible fraud, but notwithstanding fraud, money spent, still serves the central intention of alleviating poverty. Money is delivered to those in abject need.

A passing word regarding the definition of *jargon* may be appropriate. It is the manipulation of words for the express purpose of saying nothing, or, more empathically, mis-leading in order to deceive. Jargonization is the first principle in political lying. It is intentionally invoking a mis-communication. In the ever-renewed ideological battle between the Left and the right jargon passes for truth when there is no such thing, just recycled un-truth. Foremost are the terms capitalism and socialism, as to utter either is to admit to a morass of un-truth. Both are readily accused to be something that they are not. An honest definition would define each relative to the other and not either/or, or mutually exclusive. There is a spectrum between to two where each runs into the other. There is no polar, bifurcated, opposition but rather a sharing of a middle ground. No coin is single sided. Productive economic activity requires a consensus of intention between "management and labor." Without fundamental cooperation much is lost and squandered. Subject to jargonization each term becomes a spear intended for the other, a demonization of each in a self-righteous disdain. Treating each other as the enemy, jargon has carried the day and the road to civil war looms on the horizon.

Quite obviously, an economic and social policy transformation on the order of the SUBI would entail a dramatic shift in general attitude. The choices we make involve systematic assumptions that would need to be brought forward and considered in this new light. Traditional ways of thinking and believing would no longer be adequate, as probing into those assumptions would be foremost in importance. In troubled times there is offered the opportunity for such a re-evaluation. When the principles of the Old Order no longer work, when tradition runs into obvious failure, many people would naturally look elsewhere and the past would be set aside. Of course the theory of this runs squarely into the emotions of that coveted past, but people eventually die off and the new takes its place. But, being capable of rational thought, it is evident that such a change is both possible and desirable and that in a pinch reason trumps emotion. The very success of the Old has led to its downfall, similar as to how one technology gets replaced by a newer version. The intellectual tribalism that so diverts the Nation no longer serves the greater good, as its zero-sum results pits the few winners against the hoard of losers where the trajectory into the future signals fundamental strife and eventual destruction. The mere thinking about such a thing already lifts one away from those assumptions and leaves one better positioned to begin the odyssey of inclusive re-consideration. Many people would refuse such an opportunity but many more would cheerfully understand the great chance involved. Betting upon the latter, one is well poised to do better and choose a more equitable future over a tortured past, the prosperity of all over the advantage of the few.

Chapter Seven
Implementation

The political philosophy of the NUA has been presented with respect to general principle and specific policy. Obviously the *implementation* of this would impact all special interests, but the effort must be made to resist their individual intrusion. To let one interest influence the general question is to let two, then three, and then all the rest. The net gain would quickly reduce to zero. A clean break is necessary. It is better to legislate on the basis of general principle and resist the distortions of special interests. It is only then that it would be possible that the net gain is greater than nothing and only then would fundamental change for the better be possible. Something must be done and nothing less than this will do.

> The fundamental solution must originate with citizens outside Washington, for it requires nothing less than to change the political culture itself. Politics has to develop a fierce, new governing impulse to displace the old one—a skeptical perspective toward the reigning assumptions about how government is supposed to govern. Only the

people can bring this into the arena and impose it on the governors.[59]

Perhaps the most important significance of the social and political philosophy of the NUA, the agenda of the *in-between*, is that it would enhance the middle class, the great majority. The policies of both the rich and the poor do not serve the common good but only their own. The rich want to keep as much as possible and the poor want to be given as much as possible as both sidestep the rigors of productive activity. The natural result is a predictable cost to society. Only the middle class, which is based upon individual labor and the spirit of the entrepreneur, can support society as a whole.

> . . . it is plain, then, that those states are best
> instituted wherein the middle classes are a larger
> and more formidable part than either the rich or
> the poor . . . whenever the number of those in
> the middle state has been too small, those who
> were the more numerous, whether the rich or the
> poor, always overpowered them, and assumed to
> themselves the administration of public affairs . . .
> when either the rich get the better of the poor, or
> the poor of the rich, neither of them will establish a
> free state. [60]

As Aristotle says so well, the best interest is served at the middle, *in-between*.

What would be the "numbers" with such a shift to the NUA? Precision would be difficult but a simple test will do. Given any particular change, is it positive or negative with respect to the budget balance? Every change would be positive. Less military spending, a health plan that pays for itself, fewer billions on the War on Drugs, fewer unemployed and more gainfully employed, a stronger economy, less waste and pollution, more taxpayers, less cost of government and, overall, a policy of "paying your own way." While all of this may seem to be imaginary, perhaps delusion, nonetheless it is possible.

> . . . the old order is failing and people everywhere
> recognize it. The next step must be to mobilize the
> political imagination—and courage—to construct
> a new order in its place. [61]

The NUA agenda would involve comprehensive and systematic change. Many special interest groups would be encouraged to go out of existence, *for their own good*. Industries would undergo major transformation and people would be dislocated for the time being. Everyone would be a party to the consequences of this change. Everyone belongs to various special interests but equally have an essential interest in the common good, and *to this we must defer*. The enflamed emotions of partisan politics must be tempered by the insight and restraint of balanced reason. These partisans need to be marginalized, both Left and Right, to the fringes of political life through the democratic process itself. In an electoral system the majority could easily vote the special interests out of power. Many would think the deference to the common good to be unacceptable, being themselves unwilling to change, having decided that the old is better than the new. Everyone would have to weigh for themselves the benefits versus the liabilities, responsibility versus irresponsibility, common interest versus special interest, long term versus short term.

The list of trade-offs could be amplified in endless ways, but the final judgment would concern the benefits for all of a greatly expanded economic base and a balance among international relations, domestic relations, and budget and taxation. Each individual would be faced with a personal choice but, when seen within the overall context of a general improvement of society and the standard of living as a whole, it is not a mere fantasy to believe that the majority of people would choose to forgo the past and to affirm the future. There would be a resounding Yes vote for the principles and agenda of the National Union Alliance. Following the contours of the Bell Curve, this would mean that the middle sixty percent of the electorate could lead with effective authority, leaving the remaining minorities at the Left and the Right to grumble among themselves. Effective and comprehensive change could be carried forth without their intrusion.

> Nothing is likely to change until people decide
> to change it. This is a truism of democracy, but it
> has special application to the deterioration of the
> Democratic Party and, ultimately, to the deeper
> dimensions of decay in the governing processes.
> If the public's voice has been lost, it cannot be
> restored without a political party to speak for it.
> Citizens cannot hope to rediscover their connection
> to power without exercising the collective power
> that is available to them through elections. None
> of the deeper problems of government . . . whatever
> plausible solutions may exist, are likely to be
> addressed until this sort of political development
> occurs. Someone will have to invent a genuine
> political party that takes active responsibility for
> its adherents. This is an awesomely large project,
> of course, for it literally means trying to construct
> piece by piece, in the fractured modern society, the
> personal and institutional relationships that might
> draw people back into the process of democratic
> governance. [62]

A more philosophical understanding of the issues requires a look at the most deep seated and persistent error in human judgment. This concerns *the nature of causality.* This is best approached through example. The Great Pyramids of Egypt stand forth in absolute objective and material majesty. Their physical presence simply dwarfs any possible human comprehension. Yet, the *initial cause* of their existence, their conception, has nothing of the objective at all but rather is a consequence of *the agency of human subjectivity.* The Pharaoh's command willed them into existence. It is not the objective but rather the subjective that defines the possibility of their objective reality. It was only as someone's conception, someone's thought, that they were conceived and then built. The conception of the idea can only be a matter of human thinking. The implications of this are nothing short of miraculous. Our great institutions possess an objective reality that is equally overwhelming as that of the pyramids. In the same way, these structures must trace their existence back to a subjective reality that conceived of their possibility and then began the work of their objective construction and maintenance. All great organizations entail a similar intentional causality, a similar legacy of mentality. In someone's prior thinking was conceived the idea that was brought to bear in the objective dimensions of space and time. The point of this is decisive. Rather than needing to remain overwhelmed and even intimidated by these structures, standing in place as if powerless, it is possible to see that their initial causality is based in subjectivity. They are a piece of mentality and not a fact of objective reality. What was once built can be re-built, what was once constructed can be de-constructed and then re-constructed or, *mental constitution is subject to mental re-constitution.* In other words, when confronted with the overwhelming objective structures of existing social and political institutions, the seemingly unassailable impression is that nothing can be done, nothing changed, that their very objectivity is resistant to human intervention and that we are powerless to do anything at all. Nothing could be further from the truth. The force of subjectivity and self-consciousness is simply the greatest power on earth. The institutional legacy of special interests and privilege can be changed. It is within the rightful power of mentality that it can do, re-do, and do again. The unwillingness to recognize this fact is the sole reason that nothing is allowed to change. Examples abound. Cold War institutions can be changed if we so choose. Social and political institutions of irresponsible short-term special interests can be changed if we so choose. *Nothing stands in our way but ourselves.* This is the power of nothingness. It is only the inertia of believing that we cannot that obstructs the path to positive change. Simply, in a world of global institutional forces it is possible to assert the greater force of self-consciousness. We can change whatever we choose if only we choose to do so. This is the essential individual and social act of our time.

Unless the self-conscious attempt is made to do something along these lines, to do something to help ourselves overcome ourselves, the consequences are quite startling. We will not have the lucky fortune to "stumble forward" into a better world, as instead there will be a crumbling and then collapse into one that shall be worse, far worse. If we so "choose," if we choose not to choose, by default, then, we will naturally come to grief. The good and the bad are easily discerned. Stay the course of irresponsible, short-term, and special interest ideological "unthinking' and we will be lost into the eternal night of quickly forgotten history. Choose otherwise, choose fundamental consensus, and think towards the greater good, and that night turns to a renewing dawn. Choose our true selves, and not exaggerations, fictions, and caricatures of personal arrogance and disdain, and then it becomes possible to do better, much better. Perhaps, the ultimate epiphany for the individual is when that person first recognizes that one's long term and common interest is *the same* as one's short term and special interest. It is when a balance is witnessed where the person's choice is no longer dictated by the *me* but rather by the *we*, where personal action is already enclosed within the greater dimension of social well-being. The division between self and others is overcome in the recognition that selfhood achieves its greatest fulfillment in a selfless deference to the greater domains of history and community. It is at this point that the reality of abundance is able to resurrect the world. Judgments regarding economic life will no longer be the preserve of vested financial self-interest but rather based upon the greater good of all. Simply, when the central welfare of the middle 60%, the middle class, is best served, then everyone else, the lowest and the highest 20%, will be better off as well. Prosperity for all is based upon the explicit benefit of the greatest number. Self-interest then will be no longer in a position to constrict abundance into a new scarcity in order to extract yet more immediate profit. Profit will now be based upon managing *abundance* for the greater good, rather than imposing scarcities for the lesser good.

We are all party to this decision. It is assumed that the single individual can do nothing but bear witness from afar. But the matter of this fundamental transformation, the necessity of understanding one's individual interests with respect to the common good, brings the question of responsibility home to the person. The choice of one's attitude is one's own. No one can be forced to be happy with this. The big questions of war and peace become personal. One realizes that power is not a matter of political leadership but rather of individual insight. One realizes that activities at the personal level have global consequences for which one is absolutely responsible. Personal participation is required. But this need not be nearly as terrifying when one realizes that the social *community* is involved throughout.

More clearly stated in another context.

> The human race now yearns to renew itself. You can sense this everywhere. You can feel it in the air. All that people are waiting for is someone to stand up and show the way. Someone to get the ball rolling. One person to topple the first domino.

Yet let me make something clear. The era of the
single Savior is over. What is needed now is joint
action, combined effort, collective co-creation.
What is called for now is not one person only, but
a large number of humans willing to be the "one
person' in their family, in their community, in their
circle of influence, who will take on the task of
bringing about change right then, right there. In
this context one person can make a huge difference,
for it is always one person within a group or cluster
who calls forth the highest vision, who models
the grandest truth, who inspires and cajoles and
agitates and awakens and ultimately produces a
contextual fields within which collective action is
rendered possible and becomes inevitable. [63]

It would be so easy to scoff at this "idealistic nonsense" and
assure oneself that time-tested greed and self-interest will prevail
and are not to be overturned. But to scoff is to overlook one
essential fact of human nature. When given a choice, when all
things are equal, the vast majority of people would prefer the
good. It is true that as afflicted individuals, when convinced
of being met with greed and self-interest by others, people
have chosen greed and self-interest for themselves. But when
an opportunity is presented where others act in harmony with
one's own best interests, then concerted positive community
action would be the overwhelming choice. One would willingly
participate. None of this of course has ever been tried, but if
the reality of a better world were to stand on the threshold of
realization, then the great positive force of individual persons
would mature towards full strength. It is easy, assuring, and
self-righteously satisfying to say "No," but then nothing is to be
done. A "Yes" is a risk, but a risk worth taking. The good is of
course infinitely greater than nothing. Such a grand opportunity
as we have simply cannot be missed for anything. Many

short-term trade-offs will be required of the individual but the long-term benefits will easily justify the effort. The self-conscious person will find no greater satisfaction than having made his own contribution. The willing participation in the building of the good, the choosing to do one's part, is the greatest thing of all. Nothing could be more.

> Group action is what is required now. You cannot
> do this alone, nor can one charismatic leader or
> one spiritual teacher produce a miracle. The time
> for individual gurus who come along and change
> the world is over . . . The world is now ready and
> able to take such action, for group communication
> is now possible as it was never possible before. The
> whole world is now linked. The entire planet is now
> connected. [64]

How is this possible? How would it happen that the National Union Alliance would achieve political power? *Easily.* We, the people of the United States, are anticipating just such a transformation but nowhere is it seen possible to take the first step. There is a pervasive frustration with the ways and means of the existing system of political affairs. People everywhere are actively looking for an alternative.

> . . . the political status quo is also highly vulnerable
> to a concerted electoral assault from citizens. The
> rising popular resentment aimed at all elected
> incumbents demonstrates the potential for such an
> effort.[65]

A wide range of groups and coalitions already have been formed, some national in scope, which are bound by the common desire for positive change. People throughout the country are thinking and doing as best they can in order to move the system forward but success has been thwarted and painfully limited. What is needed is the articulation of general principle and specific policy with a plan of action that encompasses a move to the good and away from the partisans of privilege and self-interest. A grand alliance is already emerging into place.

> The truly difficult part would be to develop focused
> political objectives that resonate authentically with
> the army of fed-up citizens—the political ideas
> that people could call their own and would march
> behind confidently.[66]

The National Union Alliance hopes to have presented these objectives. It is a first step and possible catalyst for a second. An initial organization could be formed with the task of clarifying in detail and then presenting this program to the American people. The center 60% of the electorate, the middle class, would quickly see that their own best interests would be better served by the affirmation of the common interest that is embodied in this agenda. Great popular enthusiasm would be forthcoming. People would understand that positive change is possible and that a specific plan is being offered for all to see. Significant contributions would be forthcoming and preparations begun for the next election. Seated elected officials would see this enthusiasm and then appreciate the virtue of their "defecting" to the new party. Hoping to retain their office they would become convinced of the need to switch to the party of the National Union Alliance. Political consciousness simply would be drawn to the center and away from the rancor of ideological extremes. Traditional bases of power would be set on a new footing. New candidates would be put forth against those hoping to retain the prerogatives of the past. Fringe factions would be left to their own devices as this program of the common interest would be able to move forward on the basis of an overwhelming electoral majority. The existing legislative process has sunk to the level of a horse-trading of one pork barrel issue for another. Each group butts heads with every other so as to maintain its turf at the expense of others. Political legislation is nothing but wailing, whining, and bad manners by those who ought to know better. Nothing is allowed to change as the momentum of social and political disintegration gains velocity. Congress wallows in its own filth as the Presidency leads from the rear. The spectacle would be humorous but it simply is not all that funny. Prejudice and self-interest are dressed up in the cloth of reasoned argument but when the pretense is removed there is nothing but prejudice and self-interest. Something better is both possible and imminent. *The person must judge.* The NUA agenda is a comprehensive program of positive change. Vote Yes or No. Nothing less will do.

This agenda could be implemented in the near term for the common good of all. It will no longer do to prop up personalities in the absence of political vision. It is time to act upon a unified plan of action, a political philosophy towards a social consensus. The process of renewal then shall have begun.

> *The dogmas of the quiet past are inadequate to the stormy present. The occasion is piled high with difficulty and we must rise with the occasion. As our case is new, so we must think anew and act anew. We must disenthrall ourselves and then we will save our country.* **Abraham Lincoln**
> *...disenthrall, indeed...*

Endnotes

1 Wolf, Dick, *The Intercept*, HarperCollins Publishers, New York, 2013, p. 314.

2 Zakaria, Fareed, *The Future of Freedom*, Norton, New York, 2003, p.230.

3 Zakaria, Fareed, *The Future of Freedom*, p. 23-4.

4 Yourcenar, Marguerite, *Memoirs of Hadrian*, Farrar, Straus, and Girous, New York, 1954, p.83.

5 Zakaria, Fareed, *The Future of Freedom*, p. 171.

6 Abraham Lincoln's re-election Party in 1864 was entitled the National Union Party.

7 Plato, 215c.

8 Francis, Dick, *Proof,* Jove Books, New York, 1985, p.167.

9 Francis, Dick, *Proof,* p. 310

10 Soros, George, *The Crisis of Global Capitalism*, Public Affairs, New York, p. 211.

11 Menard, Louis, *The Metaphysical Club*, Farrar, Straus, Giroux, New York, 2001, p. 409.

12 Plato, 338a.

13 Cf., Meyer, Jack, *Alcibiades: Fact, Fiction, Farce*, ADbook Press, 2018. This is a critique of current American foreign policy from the perspective of a war between Athens and Sparta where Athens was the superpower and lost. The United States may be losing for the same reasons.

14 Wolin, Richard, *The Seduction of Unreason: The Intellectual Romance with Fascism from Nietzsche to Postmodernism*, Princeton University Press, 2004, p. 150.

15 Isaacson and Thomas, *The Wise Men*, Touchstone Books, New York, 1986, p. 648.

16 Kesey, Ken, *Sometimes a Great Notion*, Viking Press, New York, 1964, p. 228.

17 Follett, Ken, *Winter of the World*, Penguin Books, p. 700.

18 Owen, B., *The Pure Cure*, Health Digest Books, Cannon Beach, 1997, p. 73.
19 Walsch, N. D., *Conversations with God*, G.P. Putnam, New York, 1995, p. 187-8.
20 *CWG*, p. 188.
21 *CWG*, p. 90.
22 *CWG*, p. 90.
23 La Fanu, James, *The Rise and Fall of Modern Medicine*, Carroll and Graf, New York, 1999, p. 352.
24 *CWG*, p. 80-1.
25 *The Tibetan Book of the Dead*, edited by W.Y. Evans-Wentz, Oxford University Press, London, 1960, p.xv.
26 Francis, Dick, *Twice Shy*, Jove Books, New York, 1982, p. 83.
27 Schlosser, Eric, *Reefer Madness*, Houghton Mifflin, Boston, 2003, p. 61.
28 Barr, Andrew, *Drink*, Carroll and Graf, New York, 1999, p. 304. Quoted from Milton Friedman.
29 McWilliams, Peter, *Ain't Nobody's Business If You Do*, Prelude Press, Los Angeles, 1993, p. 551.
30 *Ain't Nobody's Business*, p. 190.
31 *Ain't Nobody's Business*, p.551.
32 *Ain't Nobody's Business*, p. 735.
33 *Ain't Nobody's Business*, p. 735-6.
34 Schlosser, *Reefer Madness*, p. 65.
35 *Ain't Nobody's Business*, p. 1.
36 *Ain't Nobody's Business*, p. 745.
37 Durant, Will, *Story of Civilization*, Simon and Schuster, New York, 1939, Vol. 2, p. 268.
38 Milwaukee Journal, 10/13/93, D1.
39 Gaddis, John, *The United States and the End of the Cold War*, Oxford University Press, New York, 1992, p. 10.
40 Schlosser, *Reefer Madness*, p. 108.
41 Roberts, Paul, *The End of Oil*, Houghton Mifflin Press, Boston, 2004, p. 215.
42 Roberts, Paul, *The End of Oil*, p. 217.

43 Roberts, Paul, *The End of Oil*, p. 276.

44 Roberts, Paul, *The End of Oil*, p. 294.

45 Murphy, Liam and Nagel, Thomas, *The Myth of Ownership: Taxes and Justice,* Oxford: Oxford University Press, 2002, p. 32.

46 Greider, William, *Who Will Tell the People*, Touchstone Books, New York, 1992, p. 102.

47 *Who Will Tell the People*, p. 103.

48 Murphy, Liam and Nagel, Thomas, *The Myth of Ownership* Oxford University Press, Oxford, 2002, p. 181.

49 Phillips, Kevin, *Wealth and Democracy* Broadway Books, New York, 2002, p. 311.

50 Stiglitz, Joseph, *Globalization and its Discontents*, WW Norton, New York, p. 78.

51 *Wealth and Democracy*, p. 361-2.

52 Euripides, *Oedipus at Colonus.*

53 *Memoirs of Hadrian*, p. 117.

54 Ferguson, Niall, *Colossus: The Price of America's Empire*, Penguin Press, New York, 2004, p. 270.

55 *Colossus*, p. 271.

56 Stern, Andy, *Raising the Floor, Public Affairs*, 2016, p.175.

57 Stern, Andy, *Raising the Floor, Public Affairs*, 2016, p.174.

58 Stern, Andy, *Raising the Floor, Public Affairs*, 2016, p.174.

59 *Who will Tell the People*, p. 155.

60 Aristotle, *Politics*, 1296a.

61 *Who Will Tell the People*, p. 155.

62 *Who Will Tell the People*, p. 264.

63 Walsch, Neale, *The New Revelations*, Atria Books, New York, 2002, p. 157-8.

64 *The New Revelations*, p. 313.

65 *Who Will Tell the People*, p. 268.

66 *Who Will Tell the People,* p. 269.

Index

About the Author

Jack Meyer is an unaffiliated nonacademic Husserlian interested in questions of political, historical, and philosophical merit. In 2007 he authored *The Odyssey of the Western Spirit: From Scarcity to Abundance,* 2nd edition. This traces the development of the emergence of civil society in the West. In 2009 Alcibiades: *Fact, Fiction, Farce* appeared, which is a critique of current American foreign policy from the perspective of a war between Athens and Sparta, where Athens was the superpower and lost. Much could be learned from this about our own times. He resides in Green Bay, Wisconsin.

Printed in the United States
By Bookmasters